STORIES FROM PLATO

AND

OTHER CLASSIC WRITERS

"CLASSICS FOR CHILDREN"

HESIOD, HOMER, ARISTOPHANES, OVID, CATULLUS, AND PLINY.

BY

MARY E. BURT

AUTHOR OF "LITERARY LANDMARKS," "THE STORY OF THE GERMAN
ILIAD," ETC.   FORMERLY TEACHER OF LITERATURE
COOK CO. NORMAL SCHOOL

Fredonia Books
Amsterdam, The Netherlands

Stories From Plato and Other Classic Writers:
Classics for Children

Edited by
Mary E. Burt

ISBN: 1-58963-911-1

Copyright © 2002 by Fredonia Books

Reprinted from the 1895 edition

Fredonia Books
Amsterdam, The Netherlands
http://www.fredoniabooks.com

Dedication

———

LOUIS AND STOCKTON
FRED AND HARRY
D. P. AND McA.
DON AND D. D. 3

PREFACE.

—◦◦—

"THERE is one mind common to all individual men. Every man is an inlet to the same, and to all of the same. He that is once admitted to the right of reason is made a freeman of the whole estate. What Plato has thought, he may think; what a saint has felt, he may feel; what at any time has befallen any man, he can understand."

When a thought of Plato becomes a thought to me,—when a truth that fired the soul of Pindar fires mine, time is no more.

EMERSON.

While it is good to walk among the living, it is good also to live with the wise, great, good dead. It keeps out of life the dreadful feeling of extemporaneousness with its conceit and its despair. It makes us always know that God made other men before He made us. It furnishes a constant background for our living.   It provides us with perpetual humility and inspiration.

Shakespeare has no biography ; and, much as we would like to know what happened to him in his life, I think we all feel doubtful whether we should get much of increased and deepened richness in our thought of him if what he did and said had been recorded. The poet's life is in his poems. The more profoundly and spiritually he is a poet, the more thoroughly this is true, the more impossible a biography of him becomes.

Let men like these talk to you and tell you of themselves. Being dead, they yet can speak. How good it is sometimes to leave the crowded world, which is so hot about its trifles, and go into the company of these great souls which are so calm about the most momentous things !

PHILLIPS BROOKS.

INTRODUCTION.

Two years ago I was asked by the Kindergarten Association of Chicago to read several papers at their Institutes on the adaptation of stories from classic sources to kindergartens. Leaders among kindergarteners had long before agreed that literature manufactured merely for commercial speculation had not vitality enough to meet the needs of the child. They had themselves resorted to Homer's Iliad and Odyssey, as a relief from the wearisomeness of the reading-matter of reading-books. I took the ground that teachers would derive more pleasure in their work if they were allowed a sweeping use of literature in their schools, each teacher detaching from classic or standard writings such hints and suggestions as she could use to the best advantage. I read about fifty stories which I had gleaned from Plato, Homer, Hesiod, Aristophanes, Pliny, Ovid, and other classic sources as illustrations of the material which teachers might select from the original writings.

These stories I had found useful in previous school-work, because they contained fine moral points, or else because they were poetic statements of natural phenomena which might enhance the study of natural science.

I was urged by many of my audience to publish the stories for kindergarten use. Since then it has come in my way to use the stories with children of ages varying from six to twelve years, and I am satisfied that the collection is suitable as a primary reader ; and I linger with grateful thought over the remembrance of the teachers and children, who, amid the allurements of life, could "leave the crowded world which is so hot about its trifles, and go into the company of those great souls which are so calm about the most momentous things."

Many thanks are due to the intelligent assistance of the Librarian and Attendants of the Chicago Public Library, and to the Editors of the Inter-Ocean for the " I Will " etching — symbol of the life which renews itself as well from ancient as from modern fire.

M. E. B.

New York, Dec., 1893.

CONTENTS.

———••———

STORIES FROM PLATO.

LESSON I.

A DREAM THAT CAME TRUE.

THERE was once a boy who loved to go to school, and it was no great

wonder, for he lived in a golden age and in a golden clime.

The streets of the city in which he dwelt were full of gleaming statues, all open to the air, and teachers and pupils walked and talked together a great deal out of doors, where they could see the violet tinted mountains and the shining sea.

This boy had one teacher, a remarkably wise one, who loved to gather a little circle about him on almost any corner. He did not tell his pupils anything. He merely asked them questions to set them thinking. One of his pupils said that he had to put his fingers in his ears and run away or he should grow old listening, so delightful were the lessons.

This wise teacher had a dream which was so good that perhaps we ought to know it. He dreamed that he had a beautiful white swan in his bosom.

The bird was so young that it had no feathers, but he watched it and fed it with great care. As soon as the feathers came upon it, the bird stretched its wings and flew with intrepid courage into the highest regions of air singing with inexpressible sweetness.

The teacher never doubted that the swan was his good pupil who loved to go to school, and that he should enjoy boundless fame.

Spelling.

ought   pupil   stretched intrepid
watched feathers dreamed inexpressible

Topics for discussion, language lesson, and geography lesson.

Socrates, the teacher. Life of Socrates.

Map of Greece: Athens, home of Socrates and Plato.

Socrates as a citizen, poor, contented with poverty, patriotic. Socrates in prison. The cup of hemlock.

Plato as a pupil. All of his teachers loved him. One teacher

PLATO.

finding all of his pupils gone except Plato exclaimed, "What care I who goes as long as Plato remains!" Plato's love for Socrates. Plato as a writer. He preserves the sayings of Socrates.

The Golden Age. Its meaning.

Schools in the Golden Age.

(See "Ten Boys on the Road from Long Ago to Now.")

LESSON II.

THE GOODNESS THAT IS WITHIN.

I WONDER if the children who are going to read this story or listen to it, like to get up early in the morning. I wonder if they want to be good and are so anxious about it that they cannot sleep.

I wonder if they think they can *learn* to be good, or if they believe that goodness is inside to start with and that it must grow and grow itself. Perhaps some little boy may think that he is not old enough to know these things, but we can tell better when we hear what the children say after the story is done.

It happened a long time ago that a young man wanted to be good. Yes, it was a long, long time ago, but who knows but what it may happen again some time?

He wanted so much to be good that he could not sleep and so he got up in the night and went to the house of a friend to tell him about it.

I think the friend must have been very good-natured, for he called out, "What's the news, Hippocrates?" when he heard the young man knocking with a stick on his door. "I want to be good," said Hippocrates, "and it makes me nervous and I cannot sleep. There is a teacher come to town who can teach it to me and I want you to get right up and take me to his house."

"It's too early, it isn't light yet," said the friend of the young man, "but I will get up and walk with you." So he rose and dressed for a walk and he went out into the garden and strolled around with Hippocrates until the sun was up, and then they set out to find the teacher who could teach people how to be good.

As they went along, the older

man, whose name was Socrates, said to the younger, "Do you really think, Hippocrates, that any one can *learn* to be good? Now it almost seems to me that there is good *in* every one and that it must grow from the inside until a man is all full of goodness; and that goodness is not outside of any one and so cannot be taken in from the outside." In a little while they came to the house of the teacher and they sat down to listen to what he had to say, and he told them a story, and I will tell it to you.

HOW JUSTICE CAME.

There was once a time when there were no men or women on

all the earth, but the gods lived on Mount Olympus. The time came, however, when men and animals were to be made and put on the earth; so the gods fashioned them inside of the earth out of clay and fire.

And when the gods wanted to bring these new creatures out of the earth into the light of day, they commanded two of the gods to clothe them and give to each just such kind of a mind as properly belonged to it. One of these gods was careful and always thought a long time beforehand, so that he should make no mistake, and they called him Prometheus, which means fore-thought.

The other god always did things carelessly. He never did any thinking until the mischief was done and it was too late to avoid trouble. So they called him Epimetheus, which means after-thought. And it was this mischief-maker who had the most to do with making mortals.

Epimetheus said to his brother, Prometheus, "Let me distribute clothing to men and animals, and give to each the sort of mind proper for it to have. When I have it all finished you can examine my work and see if I have done it right."

Having coaxed Prometheus and gained his permission, Epimetheus set about clothing the animals and giving them gifts of mind. He covered the dog with hair and gave him swiftness, but he did not give him the power to talk.

He covered the cat with nice soft fur and gave her strong eyes that she might see in the dark, but he did not give her the cunning, which he gave to the rat. He covered the tortoise with a shell and made it slow and patient, but he did not give it the power to climb a tree.

He covered the wolf with long hair, gave him sharp teeth and a terrible howl, but he did not give him the fidelity of the dog. He gave littleness to worms and prepared them to live in the mud or crawl on plants. He gave hoofs to horses, and to the elephant a thick skin, and covered the sheep with wool.

He kept giving and giving, until he had given everything away and yet he had not come to men. He had given everything to irrational animals. So the human race remained unadorned and Epimetheus was at his wits' end, for he did not know what to do about it.

Then Prometheus came to examine his brother's work and was much ashamed to find that every animal, except man, was clothed and provided with everything suitable, while man was naked, unshod, without any bed and without any weapons to defend himself, or any tools with which to take care of himself; and the day had arrived, when all the living things must come out to the light and live on the outside of the earth.

MINERVA.

Prometheus wondered what he could do to aid men. He knew that they must starve and freeze, if they were left in such a helpless condition.

So he went among the gods to see what he could find, that would help the poor mortals and keep them from being destroyed. In the workshop of Vulcan, the old lame blacksmith - god, he found Minerva, the goddess of Wisdom, making spears, and spindles, and other useful things.

He saw that a certain kind of wisdom came from using fire and making tools, so he stole some of the fire and some of the wisdom, too, and took them down to mortals for a present.

Then man became possessed of the wisdom, which would enable him to keep from starving and freezing, and of the power to defend himself against wild beasts.

But there was a higher wisdom, the wisdom of loving one another, which Prometheus did not bring down to man, for that wisdom was locked up and in the safe-keeping of Jupiter, the greatest of the gods.

Jupiter was so terrible, that Prometheus was afraid to go to his home, which was guarded very securely.

Prometheus had been forbidden by Jupiter to visit his home any more, because he had stolen the fire and taken it down to men; the fire belonged to the gods, and it made men godlike, to know how to use it. Old Jupiter did not want men to become godlike. He was very jealous for fear that earthly creatures might grow stronger and wiser than himself.

So all the mortals went up onto the face of the earth instead of staying inside of it, and they took some fire and the kind of wisdom which goes along with fire and teaches men how to keep themselves alive awhile. And they built altars to the gods, and made statues of the gods, and burnt incense to them, which pleased Jupiter very much, and he thought men were rather nice after all.

In the course of time men began to try to talk, and pretty soon they made words, and after a long time they could tell little stories. Then they built huts, and larger huts, and by and by they devised little houses, and larger houses, until at last they built grand palaces. They made shoes too, and beds, and cooked food, and learned to make clothes and dress themselves.

But they lived lonely lives notwithstanding, for they were scattered all over the country. They had no cities. They kept on using fire, and learned more and more wisdom all the time from using it, but this wisdom was only physical wisdom. It was outside of them and not inside, and so it did not do anything for them, except to keep them alive and flourishing.

It did not teach them how to live together. It did not exactly teach them how to live separately either, for sometimes the wild beasts would attack them in such a way and in such great numbers, that many of them were killed.

So they sought to collect themselves together, to preserve themselves from destruction, and they began to build cities. When they had built cities, and had come to live in them, and were all crowded together, they hurt one another, because they had no wisdom, except the physical wisdom that came by using fire. They were selfish, and each man took anything that he wanted, that belonged to his neighbor, and if his neighbor offended him, he kicked, and cuffed, and even killed him.

When men had lived together a little while, and had quarrelled and fought until they had almost destroyed each other, Jupiter looked down from Mount Olympus and said, "Are these the men who used to build temples for me, and burn incense, and sing songs, and praise the gods? Oh, what a shame, that they don't know how to live together without destroying one another!

I must unlock the wisdom, I have hidden away, the wisdom that teaches people how to be generous and loving. I will send this wisdom down to them, and I will call it *Justice.*

Every man shall have it inside of him, right in his heart, and he will be ashamed to hurt his brother. He will not think anything valuable that comes to him through greed.

He will not want any advantage
at all that comes through the

disadvantage or the grief of another."

Then Jupiter called Epimetheus and said to him, " There is the Wisdom of Love. Take it down and give it to men, so that they can live together in cities, and not destroy one another."   " Shall I give it to every man ? " said Epimetheus, " or to a few — just the best men ? "

" Give it to every man," said Jupiter.   " Put it right into his heart. Make it a part of him. Let it flow in his blood. Let it look out of his eyes.   Let it thrill from the ends of his fingers.

Let it speak from his tongue and in the actions of his body. And you shall make a great and everlasting law in my name," continued Jupiter, " that any man who cannot take the wisdom of love into his heart, and be ashamed of injustice, shall be put to death as a pest to the city."

So Epimetheus took the Wisdom of Love — the Justice — from Jupiter and brought it down, and made it a part of men, and now if a man has not that wisdom, he is not considered a man at all, but a sort of beast.

And every good man wants every other man to be good. The mother wants the little child to be good; the nurse, the teacher, and the father, all try to make the children good, and when people are bad they are punished, in hopes that they will become good.

And now you may tell me whether you think goodness is outside of you or inside. And you may tell me whether you think Hippocrates learned to be good by going to the teacher, or whether he carried his goodness in his heart all the time.

Spelling.

anxious	distribute	flourishing
believe	elephant	clothe
mischief	physical	examine
patient	quarrelled	neighbor
tortoise	good-natured	possessed
generous	fashioned	Olympus
enough	irrational	Jupiter
happened	separately	mortals

Hip poc′ ra tēs (ēz)   Pro me′ theus (ūse)

Ep i me′ theus (ūse)

Note to Teachers.

(See "The Protagoras.") Plato's object in "The Protagoras" was doubtless to display the superior skill of Socrates in handling a discussion. Protagoras starts out with the assumption that virtue can be taught, but he ends by proving that it is innate. The motive of Socrates is quite different from that of Plato or Protagoras. It was to teach the importance of growth through self-activity. This is what Froebel taught, and the two philosophers clasping hands across the centuries are worthy to be classed together as great educators for this reason.

Topics for discussion and language lesson.

The patience of Socrates. Did he take the best way to teach the young man goodness?

SOCRATES.

Self-activity. Physical growth. Do trees grow from within or from without? Moral growth.

Relation between the desire to be good and the practice of being good.

LESSON III.

FOR THE LITTLE BOY WHO WILL NOT SAY "PLEASE."

ONCE in a while there is a little boy who does not know how to say "please" and "thank you." I have even seen one who did not seem to care for any one or respect anybody. So I will tell you a story which shows how necessary it is that people should be respectful.

JUPITER.

There was a time when all the men living on the earth were

disrespectful. They never said "please" nor "thank you," and they grabbed everything away from others, and no one cared for any one else.

At that time men were double. They had two faces, two pairs of arms, two pairs of legs, four hands, and four feet. Their bodies were round like a ball, and when they walked they rolled over and over like a wheel, or more like a boy turning somersaults, heels over head, head over heels, hand over hand, they went bumping along in a most ridiculous fashion.

They were twice as strong as they are now, and they could run twice as fast, and climb any tree like a cat. They were very fierce, too, and so saucy to the gods that old Jupiter was almost afraid they would climb Mount Olympus and put the gods to flight. He trembled on his throne when he saw how strong and daring they were.

So Jupiter called Apollo and told him to take each mortal and cut him right down through the middle so that he should have only one pair of legs and arms; and to smooth him out and pull the skin around him and tie it up and set his face straight and make him walk upright on two legs, so that he would be one man instead of a double man.

Jupiter told Apollo to teach him to be respectful also, and to instruct him that if he did not treat the gods respectfully and love his fellow-men he would have him sliced right in two again so that he would have to go hopping around on one leg and have only one arm, one eye, and half a nose.

Now, when men began to walk on two legs and to try to help themselves with two arms they began to feel very lonesome for that other half that had always been with them, and they kept thinking about the other half, and that is the way men learned to care for each other and to think about other folks instead of thinking all the time about themselves.

I am afraid that the little boy who will not say "please" will lose half of himself some time if he does not learn to be polite and kind.

Spelling.

necessary　respectful　double　　grabbed

A pol'lo　　Ju'pi ter　ridiculous　smooth

Note to Teachers.

(See Plato's "Symposium.")

Topics for discussion.

The belief of the ancients in Jupiter and Apollo and other gods. Mount Olympus. Politeness. Saucy children losing their best friends ; the truth in the story.

LESSON IV.

THE GIFT OF THE MUSES.

IT happened on a warm day in summer that a man and a boy lay down under a tree. There was a fountain of cold water close by. It ran over a grassy slope among images and statues which showed it to be a fountain sacred to the water-nymphs.

There was a choir of grass-hoppers in the tree and they added their music to the summer-like harmony of the hour.

The man was a famous wise man and he said to the boy, " The grasshoppers are singing over our heads as is their custom in the heat of the day.

They are talking with each other and appear to be looking down on us. If they should see us falling asleep, as most men do at noontime, they would think us indolent of mind, and they would laugh us to scorn.

They would say, some slaves or other had come to listen to their music and that they had gone to sleep like sheep by the side of the fountain.

But if they see us talking together and sailing by them as if they were sirens who had lost their power of enchanting, the gift which they have from the Muses, to confer upon men, they may perchance bestow upon us."

"What is this gift from the gods?" said the boy. "I have never heard of it."

"It is not proper," replied the man, "that a lover of wisdom should not have heard of these things. Know, then, that it is said that these grass-hoppers were men before the Muses were born. But when the Muses came they invented song, and some of the men who lived at that time, were so overcome by the pleasure of listening to their singing, that they forgot to eat and drink.

Thus they died thoughtlessly from starvation. From their bones the race of grass-hoppers sprang up and the Muses gave them this gift, that they could live without food from the time of their birth, and that they could sing all the time without food or drink until they died.

And the Muses gave them another gift, that after death they should go to the Muses and live with them, and inform each Muse by whom she was honored on the earth. So now they tell the goddess of the dance who honors her and they make the dancers dear to that goddess. And they tell the goddess of love all about lovers. And so on with all the rest.

But the goddess of wisdom and the goddess of learning they tell of those that pass their lives in speaking wisely. And upon these people most of all, the Muses pour forth their heavenly gifts. Therefore, my boy, let us not sleep lest we loose the gift of the Muses."

"No, indeed," said the boy, "let us talk of wise things and not sleep."

Spelling.

nymphs grass-hoppers harmony indolent starvation enchanting statues sirens

Topics for discussion.

The Muses. The ancient idea of nymphs living in streams and trees.

What Socrates means to teach in this story.

(See Plato's "Phædrus.")

LESSON V.

WHY THE QUARRELSOME MEN WERE LOCKED OUT OF BIRD CITY.

THERE was once a beautiful city where for a long time people were good and brave and happy. They sang sweet songs, told pleasant stories, built great temples and offered sacrifices to the gods. But it came about as time passed on, that they grew selfish, each man desiring the things that belonged to some other man, and when he could not get them he went to law about it to make the other man give them up.

There were two men living in the beautiful city who grew tired

of all this wrangle and made up
their minds that they would go off
to a pleasanter place. So each of

them bought a bird; one bought a magpie and the other a jackdaw, to show them the way to a better land.

They travelled about for many days, tramping up and down, watching every motion of the birds, so that they might find the way to the happy land.

At last the birds flew straight up into the air and of course the two travellers had to follow them. When they had gone up far enough they came to a country where they found a king who had once been a man and had lived in the beautiful city. But he too had become tired of seeing people quarrel, and had run away up to bird-land where he had changed into a hoopoe and lived in peace.

The two travellers came to the door of King Hoopoe and knocked very loudly, but no one answered

them, so they cried out at the top of their voices, "Hoop! Hoop! Hoopoe!" and the king's servant came to the door.

The servant was a very large bird, but he was frightened when he saw the travellers, for he was afraid that they were a pair of bird-catchers, so he told them that they had better be off or the birds would get after them and put them to death.

This scared the travellers, and they told him that they were changing into birds themselves and asked him who he was. The servant replied that he was once a slave and lived with his master in the beautiful city. But when Hoopoe ran away from the quarreling people and came up to bird-land, he came too, and was changed into a slave-bird, in order that he might still wait upon his master.

"King Hoopoe has not forgotten that he was once a man," said the slave-bird, "and sometimes he longs to eat bread and honey or porridge. So I bake bread for him and mix porridge when he wants it."

"I wish you would call your master out so that we can talk with him," said one of the travellers.

"I do not like to do that," said the slave-bird. "He has been eating a bowl of berries, and a plate of worms, and now he is taking a little rest."

The travellers insisted, however, that King Hoopoe should be called to the door, and the slave-bird was obliged to call him, and the royal Hoopoe came out. He had a tremendous beak and crest, but few feathers and was very ridiculous in his appearance. Hoopoe received the strangers kindly and asked them why they had come to bird-land, so they told him that they had run away from the beautiful city where there were so many quarrels, and had come to bird-land where they hoped to build a city up in the air, between heaven and earth.

"Men live on earth," said the travellers, "and the gods live up in the heavens, and if we build a city just between them, we shall be masters of both. The gods live on the smoke which comes up to them from the sacri-

fices which men burn on their
altars.

If we build our city between
them we shall starve the gods, and
then they will be obliged to come
down and beg us to be kind to them
and they will pay us taxes."

King Hoopoe forgot for a little
while that he had left the beautiful
city to get away from quarrels, and
thought the travellers were very
smart men, and that it would be a
clever idea to build the city. Then
he called all of the birds together
to tell them what the strangers had
proposed, and they came running
and scrambling with a great clatter,
crying, "Where are the men who
want to build a city in bird-land?

Whee! Whaw! Where? Where?
What? What? What? What?"

At first the birds looked fierce
and angry. I think they were
afraid that the travellers meant to
catch their king and carry him off.
They formed in ranks like soldiers
and acted as if they intended to
tear the strangers to pieces.

The travellers seized some huge
kettle-covers and held them up
before their faces so that the birds
should not dash at their eyes with
their strong beaks. But old King
Hoopoe told them to stand back
and treat the men kindly since
they were friends.

Then the travellers told all the
birds that if they would help to

build the city they should rule over the gods. "It is only right," said they, "for you are older than the gods and the older ones should rule over the younger. It is a well known fact," continued the strangers, "that birds are older than the earth even. For the lark had no place to bury his father when he died, because the earth had not then been invented. And it is true, too, that mankind worshipped the birds once.

But the gods overcame the birds, and now Jupiter always appears carrying an eagle, Minerva an owl, Apollo a hawk, and so on." The birds listened with great interest to the flattering speeches of the travellers, and asked how they should make Jupiter and his Olympian host surrender to the birds. "This is the way to do it," said the travellers. "We will build the city and put very strong walls around it and make forts to defend it. Then we will starve out the gods by keeping from them the incense which comes up from their altars on earth. They will dispatch messengers down to earth to find out why men do not send up any more incense. We will capture their messengers and keep them until the gods come down and offer to pay us tribute.

And we will send a messenger down to men and tell them that

every time they offer a sacrifice to Venus they must feast the sparrows with grain; every time they offer gifts to Neptune they must feast the ducks and drakes with barley, and so on until all the birds are fed.

And if the people on the earth agree to do this we will offer to equip an army of owls to destroy the grass-hoppers that eat up their vines, and an army of thrushes to destroy the worms which spoil their figs, and so with all the other insects which injure their crops; and we will help them further by sending the sea-mew to guide their ships over the stormy sea, and there is a bird that can point out to them where gold and silver is hidden away in the earth."

The birds were well pleased with this arrangement and they went to work with a right good will to build the city. There were thirty thousand cranes who brought stones from Africa in their gizzards, and the curlews worked them into shape. The mud-larks and the sand-martins mixed mortar, and the water-birds brought water to soften the mortar. The crows and pigeons helped the masons; and the geese, all barefoot, trampled down the mortar and put it into hods, while an army of ducks climbed up the ladders with the hods, and used their little feet for trowels to smooth down the plaster.

The wood-peckers were the carpenters and they made a great clatter hammering away hard at work. When the city was all

finished they put jackdaws upon the towers to watch over the city and catch any of the messengers from the gods who might be sent down to earth to demand sacrifices of men.

It was not long before a messenger appeared in sight. The beautiful Iris with her rainbow-robes came flying down, and not knowing that the birds had built a city in the air, she flew right into their midst. The birds were greatly excited. They sent an army of ten thousand hawks, and twenty thousand hobby-hawks and great numbers of vultures, falcons, ospreys, eagles and other birds to catch her.

On every side there was a rushing and whizzing sound as the birds flew hither and thither searching for her. The travellers were the first to see her and they cried out: "Halt! Stop this instant! Who are you? Where do you come from?"

"Why, I come from Mount Olympus, to be sure," said Iris, "and I am sent by father Jupiter to command mortals to sacrifice to him."

"Which of the city-gates did you enter? Did any of the bird-masters examine you and let you pass through our city? Ho, guards! take her and lead her to prison!"

When Iris heard this she was indignant and told them that she did not know there was any bird-city, so the travellers and the birds advised her to go back to Mount Olympus and tell father Jupiter that he must pay the birds a tribute of money whenever he sent a messenger to earth. And they told Iris that they would steal her beautiful rainbow-colors away from her if she ever dared to come that way again.

The unhappy goddess flew back to Mount Olympus and repeated to Jupiter all that had happened. It was a sad time for Jupiter and the rest of the Olympian gods. They waited long and patiently for the smoke of sacrifices to come to them.

At last when they began to starve they sent Hercules and Neptune down to promise the birds that they should be well paid if they would allow the smoke to come up to the gods from the altars on earth.

And they promised to give the birds water for their tanks and rainy weather, or dry weather, or

any sort of weather for which they had a mind to ask. They gave another promise, too, that one of the travellers who had taught the birds to build the city should have a beautiful goddess for a wife. The birds received old Neptune and Hercules very kindly and agreed to allow the gods to have their incense, and they had a gay wedding for the traveller and the goddess, and all the birds and all the gods became good friends.

Now when the quarrelsome men down on the earth saw the good fortune of the travellers they were wild with envy.

Each man wanted to build a city and become very rich and very famous all in a minute. They wanted to go up to bird-land and live in the bird-city and have the gods pay them taxes.

And they were so greedy and so conceited that they even thought they ought to have goddesses for wives, although they were so dreadfully common that they could not have told a goddess from a pig with a ring in its nose.

These quarrelsome men said to themselves, "If we can get into the bird-city we will live in the bird-palaces which are much grander than our houses, and after awhile we will kill all the birds or drive them down to earth to build their nests in trees."

So the quarrelsome men sent a messenger up to the bird-city with flattering messages and this is what he said: "Oh, beautiful birds, the people on earth have sent you a gold medal to show how much they admire you. And you, oh travellers, you who have become the founders of this great city, you do not know how much you, too, are admired and watched. Birds and travellers are all the fashion.

The people on earth do everything just as the birds do. They rise with the lark, they scratch and scrabble, they pick and peck, and they all wish for wings to fly. They try to sing like birds and there are thousands of them who are preparing to come up to live in your bird-city, so that they can get wings and claws, marry goddesses, and collect taxes from the gods."

But King Hoopoe said to the city-guards: "Lock the gates. We do not want quarrelsome men to come up here. They will quarrel with the birds as they quarrel with each other, and rob them of their homes and kill them. They will quarrel with our friends, the gods, and keep their incense from them, and they will forget to worship them."

So the gates of the bird-city were locked and the quarrelsome men had to stay on earth. But the happy birds went singing and flying wherever they pleased. Sometimes they flew off into the blue sky

among the clouds and rainbows.
Sometimes they flew down to earth
to destroy grass-hoppers and worms,
or to eat grain from the altars of
the gods.

Sometimes they flew up to
Mount Olympus and gave lovely
concerts, singing sweet melodies in
chorus before the gods. And the
gods were pleased to hear their
sweet songs and told them that the
heavens were more beautiful because they were there. But their
happiest days were spent with their
mates and young ones in their
pretty homes in bird-land.

And now, I am sure, we all feel
sorry for quarrelsome men, because
they are shut out of the bird-city.

Spelling.

sacrifices	obliged	thousands
desiring	pigeons	surrender
straight	palaces	arrangement
curlews	appearance	incense
conceited	received	trowels
forgotten	fierce	melodies

Note to Teachers.

The poet Aristophanes, "The Father of Comedy" (430 B.C.) doubtless made a great point against litigation and unpatriotic ambitions in his comedy "The Birds." The art of good citizenship is the underlying lesson in the drama. (See "The Birds," Frère's translation.)

Topics for discussion.

The art of living in communities. Who is the best citizen? Does a pupil in the school-room show himself a good or bad citizen?

Is a good citizen anxious to have better things for himself than other people have? The ancient idea that what belonged to the state should be better than what belonged to the private individual. The man who was despised because his house was finer than public buildings. Would we rather live in fine houses or see fine public buildings now-a-days? Real patriotism. Athens 430 B.C. Neptune, god of the water. Hercules. Iris.

(See "Gods and Heroes.")

Science lesson.

Comparison of the birds in this story with birds as the pupil has observed them. Their habits of building. The Hoopoe. The Curlew.

The rainbow. Why naturally considered a messenger from Heaven to Earth.

(See Jackman's "Nature Studies.")

Note to pupils.

The "Life of Alcibiades," as given by Plutarch, would be interesting home-reading in connection with this story.

LESSON VI.

MEMORY AND HER BEAUTIFUL DAUGHTERS.

ONE might suppose that a great king sitting on a throne high up among the clouds ruling the world must have everything that heart could wish. Just think how grand one would feel to throw the lightning from cloud to cloud and send the thunder rolling through the sky. Fire-crackers and skyrockets would seem quite tame after that.

King Zeus grew very tired of it sometimes. He had it in his power to make the earth glad with warm sunshine, but he grew tired of that, too. He could make the earth dreary and sad with frost and cold. He could crush giants under

ZEUS.

great rocks, and rule over the gods, and banquet on nectar and ambrosia, but he became weary of all these things. And the reason why he grew tired was that he kept thinking all the time about the events that were taking place just before him.

He looked down on the earth and saw men quarreling with one another and he thought about that. His wife, Juno, teased him, and he thought about that. His fellow gods on Mount Olympus played tricks on him and he played tricks on them and all was vexation. It is no wonder he wearied of looking at and thinking of what was going on just around him.

He wished that he might remember the beautiful things of the past and that he might know the good things that would happen after awhile, so he made a mighty wish in his heart and this is what it was.

He wished that there would come to him some lovely daughters who would dance about him and keep him thinking of the beautiful things which had happened long ago, so that he would forget his troubles. And he wanted them to sing of the wonderful things that were going to happen some time in the future.

After awhile it all happened just as he desired. There came a beautiful goddess, whose name was Memory, leading nine grown-up daughters to him that they might please him by causing him to think of the pleasant things of the past and to anticipate the pleasures of the future.

King Zeus was so happy when he saw the pretty maidens before him that he forgot to think of the quarrels on earth and other disagreeable matters. He could do nothing but admire his daughters and tell them how glad he was that they had come to him. They danced before him and sang songs to him and he gave them a whole mountain for their home, and there they lived, bathing in the violet-tinted fountains, and dancing around the altar which was sacred to their father.

They burnt incense to Zeus on this altar and they taught people to sing songs praising him. There was a beautiful flying horse which came to their home on the top of this mountain. Once, when it was very thirsty, it struck the side of the mountain with its hoof, and a fountain of clear cold water sprang up, so that the winged horse could drink.

The nine daughters of King Zeus used to pet the flying horse and give him delicious food and he was not afraid of them. He was a gentle creature and flew away from cross and ugly people, but he came to poets and musicians. They never tried to yoke him down to a plough to do dirty work, but gave him pleasant burdens to bear. He often carried their music up to Mount Olympus. So it is no wonder that the nine daughters of Zeus loved him.

It was wonderful the comfort Zeus took in his pretty daughters. When he saw that they were wise and good and could drive away cares, he gave them the power to shed honeyed dew upon the lips of all babies who were going to grow up and become kings or wise men. This was a greater gift to any babe than to give him gold or silver, for he was sure to speak gentle words and make wise laws.

And Zeus gave the power also to his daughters to take sorrow out of the heart and make all sad people forget their troubles. I do not suppose you quite believe my story, but perhaps if you will stop to think how dreadful it would be to forget all your kind friends and all the pleasant things that have happened to you, you may agree with me that Memory has beautiful daughters.

And perhaps you will want to learn many poems and stories while you are very young, so that you can think of them when you grow older and get tired of daily storm-clouds and every-day cares.

Spelling.

Memory disagreeable daughter delicious nectar ambrosia honeyed plough

Zeus (Zūse)

Note to Teachers.

See the "Theogony" of Hesiod (800 B.C.).

Topics for discussion and language lesson.

The use and abuse of the memory. Need of cultivating the memory. The nine Muses. The greatest of them. Zeus (or Jupiter, — Zeus-pater), the same.

Science lesson.

The lightning. Ancient and modern ideas of it. Electricity. Telegraph, telephone, and so on.

LESSON VII
A CLOUD AND A FOUNTAIN.

A GREAT white cloud went sailing off into the sky on a bright summer day. It met a breeze which blew it away to the north where it became quite cold. So it shrugged its shoulders and pulled its flying, feathery robes close together which caused it to become a trifle heavier and it fell a little lower.

Then an east wind caught it and drove it against the side of a mountain and held it there, squeezed tight up against the mountain as you squeeze your wet sponge against a slate. Its little fleecy particles were pressed into round drops and the greater part of the beautiful cloud had become rain, but what was left escaped from the cruel east wind and flew away.

The little rain drops tried to keep together as they fell on the side of the mountain, so they all joined hands and ran along a little way until they came to a great queer basin in the rock that was full of water. They leapt into this basin, but it was so crowded with other drops of water that they were pushed out again, and so they kept hold of hands and ran dancing down the side of the mountain in a little channel which they found, where a stream used to run.

Now it happened that a shepherd boy had been lying all of this time in a grassy field at the foot of the mountain, tending his sheep. He had been looking up into the sky watching the great white cloud over his head. It did not look like a cloud to him, but like a beautiful white horse with wings flying about in the heavens.

Sometimes it seemed to fly closer to him and sometimes it seemed to fly away. And he believed that it really was a flying horse, so he kept watching and watching it. When the wind blew it against the side of the mountain, the horse appeared to be thirsty and the boy believed that he saw him strike the earth with his hoof.

When the stream came dancing down the side of the mountain, the shepherd lad said to himself, "surely the beautiful flying horse was very thirsty and struck the earth with his hoof, and I do not doubt that he broke open a fountain and it has sprung out of the ground and is running down the mountain." Then he climbed up the side of the mountain and sure enough, he found the queer rocky basin with a fountain jetting up from it, sending the little stream down the mountain. Then the boy went home driving his sheep, and he called his brother and other shepherd lads together and told them of the strange sight which he really believed that he had seen.

And the friends of the shepherd boy believed as he did that the fountain came because the horse was thirsty and struck the ground with his hoof. So they called the spring "The fountain of the Horse," and I think if we were shepherd lads watching the clouds off on a lonely mountain, we might imagine even more wonderful things about them than has been told in this story.

Spelling.

feathers   believed   particles   channel
shepherd   fleecy   appeared   imagine

Note to Teachers.

See Hesiod's "Theogony." This story of Pegasus and the fountain of Hippocrene is told also by Ovid and Hawthorne. In connection with it, it is well to let the pupil read "Pegasus in Pound" by Longfellow, or "Pegasus harnessed to a Plough" by Schiller. The story has always been a favorite in literature. See Cox's "Manual of Mythology," or Gayley's "Classic Myths in English Literature."

Topics for discussion.

Formation of clouds. Formation of springs. Cloud-forms. What we see in the clouds. Formation of myth stories from nature truths, a natural process. Pastoral poetry.

Geography.

Mount Helicon and its vicinity, and also Corinth and its neighborhood. The story is attached to both localities.

LESSON VIII.

THE GIFT OF POESY.

THERE was once a learned man named Valmiki who loved God and his fellow men; and he took up his abode in a wild and lonely forest that he might learn what was right by thinking. Just as a traveller climbs a mountain to get a view of the whole country about him that he need not go astray, so did Valmiki seek the temple of nature that by thinking over all he had met and seen, he should know people better and be able to serve them more acceptably.

The forest where he dwelt was very beautiful. There were lofty tamarind and mango trees where birds of a thousand hues flashed to and fro, and the ground was strewn with rich blossoms whose incense perfumed the air.

Here Valmiki lived all alone for many years praising the great Creator and contemplating how it might best come about that all men should be taught the universal brotherhood of all living creatures.

The inhabitants of the woods learned to love the kind man who lived on roots and berries, and after awhile they came to him when they were in trouble. Even the timid gazelles which came in flocks to the stream to quench their thirst would look up into his face as much as to say, "We wish you good evening, Valmiki."

The glow-worm and the fire-fly shed their lights around him in the dark lest he should tread upon a poisonous plant or serpent, and the tigers and other beasts crept out of sight. At the sound of his steps the flowers opened their corollas and smiled, saying, "Are you ill, Valmiki? there is a healing power for you in my root."

At length as Valmiki sat at the door of his hut one evening, there came the messenger of the gods and said to him, "If men learn to love the great universal nature, if they learn to love the good and the true, it must be through hearing stories of heroic lives; is this not so, Valmiki?"

"Not so," said Valmiki; "if man learn to be truly noble, he must have one great hero to follow, one who, although poor and weak and suffering, has done generously and well, endured sorrow without bitterness, controlled his passions, dealt kindly with all living creatures. One such example man needs—to follow."

"There is such a hero," said the messenger, "but what poet is there who is great enough to tell his virtues to the people in a poem which all men shall love to read,—a poem so great that men shall believe it and shall seek to follow the life of the hero?

I charge you, Valmiki," said the messenger of the gods, "by your love of man, never rest until you have discovered this poet." With this the heavenly messenger returned to his celestial home. Then Valmiki was sorely troubled and said to himself, "How shall I find such a poet in this solitary forest? To be clean and pure is the great wisdom. I will lave my body in the water and keep my soul pure, and perhaps the great God will give me clear perception that I may find the gifted poet, worthy to write the song of the hero."

So saying, the hermit prepared to bathe himself in the river, but as he lingered on the brink, he beheld on the opposite shore two herons of surpassingly beautiful plumage. It was the season when the buds are bursting forth from the trees and all Nature thrills with love. There is at this time more beauty in the world; all living things are radiant with ardor; the colors of the trees and flowers are of a richer dye, and the birds break forth into song.

"We thank Thee, O Supreme Author of life!" exclaimed these herons of marvelous plumage, "for the gift of lustrous waters, for the wings which give us empire over the realms of air, and above all for the love which we find in each other."

But while these harmless birds expressed joyously their thanksgiving, the arrow of some pitiless hunter hissed through the startled air, and, piercing the poor breast of one of the winged lovers, destroyed the life that had just reached its happiest moment. Then the mournful shrieks of the bereaved heron, which beheld his innocent mate stretched there dabbled in blood, saddened the shores of the lake and saddened, too, the kind heart of the hermit. "O cruel hunter!" he cried, "mayst thou attain no glory in the eternal revolution of years, since thou hast not feared to strike this heron in its supreme happiness."

As the bubbling springs gush from the soil, so leapt the words from his heart. And as the sound of flowing waters mellows itself into harmony, so did his grief for the desolate bird sing itself into measure, swaying his thoughts to and fro with a musical, dreamy movement, as the breeze blows forward and back the boughs of the sad weeping-willow.

The rhythm of his lamentations rang in his ears while he bathed in the limpid waters, and even when he had left the crystal lake the enchanting measure still haunted him. Against his will he kept repeating it over and over, until, sorely puzzled and distressed, he fancied that some charm had bewitched him.

That day the greatest of the gods came to visit the meek hermit. Valmiki reverently bowed himself to the earth, his hands clasped above his head as is befitting the presence of one worthy of honor, and he begged the most illustrious of the gods to inform him of his pleasure.

Then Brahma, the god, said: "The fame of your wisdom and holiness has reached me, O Hermit! I long to hear you speak of virtue and knowledge, and of the grave contemplations that have absorbed

your mind while you have lived in
this forest." Valmiki tried to tell
his illustrious guest of the way to
encourage man to become noble
and generous and pure. But his
tongue could only repeat the
musical words in which he deplored
the death of the heron.

Valmiki was abashed and con-
fused and he trembled before the
most ancient of the gods, fearing
that Brahma would think that he
meant to mock him. But the
eternal Brahma smiled and said,
"Happy art thou, Valmiki, who
hast found favor in the sight of the
ardent goddess of eloquence! The
divine quality of pity has drawn to
thee the kiss of the goddess of

harmony. Up, then, oh man, who hath tasted an immortal's love, and speak forth the divine breath which inspires thee! Sing to the listening ages the wondrous story of the great hero whose beauty shall not fade till the stars grow dim in the sky."

Thus did Valmiki receive the divine gift of poesy in exchange for tears of pity, because there dwelt in his heart the feeling of universal brotherhood.

Spelling.

Creator	poisonous	perception
contemplating	corollas	radiant
universal	messenger	ardor
habitation	solitary	supreme
wondrous	bewitched	receive

Brāhma   Val mi′ ki (Vahl mē′ kē)

Note to Teachers.

This story is taken from "The Ramayana" (Rah mä ah' nah) or the great epic of India, "The Deeds of the Hero Rama." (See Richardson's *Iliad of the East*, from which the story is adapted. See also "Hindoo Literature" by Elizabeth Reed.)

Topics for discussion.

The necessity of simplicity if one would become wise. "Give thyself time to learn something new and good, and cease to be whirled around." Temptations of children in school to go to too many parties and places of amusement.

The main point of the story, the quality of tenderness. The heart that can easily sympathize has already the Gift of Poesy. Contrast Valmiki with Skipper Ireson with his "hard heart." "Vulgarity is lack of feeling." Ruskin.

Bird hunting. The trade in birds' wings and bodies. "What is a bird without its song?" Compare the poet who loves the bird for its song with the woman who wears the dead song-bird on her hat. Which admires the bird the more? Which shows the finer feeling?

LESSON IX.

THE POCKETS OF GOOD AND BAD DEEDS.

WHEN Jupiter watched the earth and did what he could to make men happy, he noticed that, while they wore cloaks and coats, they had no pockets; nor had they any record of their good and bad deeds.

So this all-wise father made them two pockets, one at each end of a long scarf which they might hang around their necks to hold their good and bad actions.

At first the people were delighted and wore the pockets dangling where every one might see them. But by and by the pocket that held the bad actions grew so large, and the one that held the good actions looked so flat, that most of the people grew ashamed and did not like to carry them.

But Jupiter said they must carry them, and this is the way they managed: they covered the pocket of the good deeds with ornaments, until it looked large and beautiful and full, and they hung it in front where everybody could see it.

But the pocket of the bad deeds they hung underneath the cloak, where no one could see it and

where it might grow very fat and
yet cause them no shame.

Spelling.

dangling cloaks ornaments underneath
actions   cause   delighted   actions

Note to Teachers.

This story is from Catullus, an early Latin poet. Translated by
Miss Bird Warder.

Topics for discussion.

Modesty. Honesty. Self-respect.
Main point of the story. Vanity. "Putting the
best foot forward."

LESSON X.

A BUTTERFLY STORY.

PSYCHE was the daughter of a great and powerful king, and she was very beautiful. The fame of her beauty awoke the jealousy and hatred of Venus, the goddess of love, and she

PSYCHE.

began to think of a plan by which she could get rid of her rival.

So Venus told her little son, Cupid, to visit the princess and send one of his darts through her heart, that she might be inspired to love some common man.

Cupid took his bow and arrows and went to the home of the princess, intending to obey his mother. But when he saw the little maiden, he thought only of her beauty, and resolved to carry her off to a happy valley where he could have her for a play-fellow.

Then he took her away to a fairy palace in a vale of paradise, where they spent many happy hours together without fear or care.

But there was one drawback to their enjoyment. Psyche was not permitted to look at her little comrade with her mortal eyes; she could only see him with the eyes of the soul. Even this would not have troubled her, if her envious sisters had not continuously urged her to look at him and find out who he was.

Yielding to the temptation, she took a lamp one night and stole into the room where Cupid lay asleep, and what was her surprise, when she saw Cupid, the god of love.

She was so alarmed at the discovery she had made that she let a drop of hot oil fall on his shoulder.

He awoke, and finding that she had disobeyed his express command, left her alone to weep in solitude and despair, while he returned to his mother. Then Psyche set out to find her lost playmate and she wandered over many lands, searching for him everywhere.

At last she came to the palace where his mother lived, and begged to see her little friend. But Venus made a servant of her and gave her hard work to do. After awhile the goddess sent her down to the infernal regions under the earth where lived dread Pluto and his bride, to get a box of beauty's ointment.

This was a great task but Psyche took the box back to Venus and sweetly opened it for her, that the goddess might become more beautiful than ever. But the ointment had such a powerful odor that Psyche fainted and fell to the floor.

Cupid could no longer resist her faithful love for him and ran to her help and brought her back to life. The anger of Venus was appeased since by using the ointment

CUPID.

she could become as beautiful as Psyche. She had not now cause to be jealous any longer. So she told Cupid not to shun Psyche any more, and their marriage was celebrated in the presence of the gods with great rejoicings.

Roses were scattered before them and a rose-tree grew up near them, for the rose is a symbol of the beauty of love.

It is said that Psyche (the soul) gave her name to the butterfly, because, like the butterfly, when freed from its chrysalis in which it had been imprisoned, it wafted its way through the light, soaring above earth.

And now, when artists paint a picture of Psyche, they give her the wings of the butterfly, because they are beautiful and because the soul seeks the freedom of the air; and they put links on her ankles to denote that the soul may be chained by love.

Sometimes they paint Cupid riding on a lion, to show that love makes people courageous, and they give him the lyre to play upon, because love produces harmony. And Hope is sometimes painted as a beautiful maiden standing before them, holding a lily in her hand, because a lily is the symbol of the purity of a soul wedded to love.

Spelling.

envious   fielding   disobeyed   paradise
celebrated   Pluto   maiden   mortal
Psyche (sī′ kē)

Topics for discussion.

Changes of the butterfly and other insects.
Why the ancients made this story.
In what way it is a nature story.
Ethical meaning.

LESSON XI.

THE MOUNTAIN THAT LOVED A WHITE WAVE.

THERE is a huge moun-tain standing down by the blue sea. It has stood there ages and ages and is just as firm on its base as ever. It is covered over with shaggy woods and it has a great eye in the middle of its fore-head, a large fiery eye.

Perhaps we ought to call it a mouth instead of an eye, for it grumbles and mumbles and mutters dreadful things.

The mountain carries a mighty

fire in its bosom and when it is not asleep it hurls rocks far out into the sea or down into the valley at its foot.

There are rivers running down the mountain. They gather red sand from the red rocks as they go dashing along so that they look like red rivers. They run to meet the white waves of the sea, and the white waves come rushing up to receive them as if they were very welcome visitors.

When the winds blow, the old mountain looks over the waters and if it isn't blind, it must see hundreds of white waves come frolicking up until they dash on the shore at its base.

If the grand old mountain had a heart in his bosom as well as a raging fire, how he would love the blue sea with its hundreds of white waves sporting like water-nymphs on dolphins' backs. It must be that the old mountain did love the waves, or how could people have thought of the story which they told about him.

Old Nereus, they said, was a grand old sea-god, a servant to Neptune, who dwelt in the waters, and he had a hundred daughters who lived in a splendid cave at the bottom of the sea.

When the winds blew and the dolphins rolled sporting on the waves, these sea-nymphs came up to ride about on their backs and enjoy the rocking of the billows. Now one of these nymphs was named Galatea, and she was very white, as white as marble. And she combed her hair while she swam around basking in the sunshine. There was a great giant standing on the shore. He had one vast fiery eye in the middle of his fore-

GALATEA AND CYCLOPS.

head. He was a shaggy monster who muttered and mumbled and threw great stones when angry.

He looked out upon the waters and saw the beautiful Galatea with

her white robes and her white face
surrounded by her hundred sisters.
When the rough old giant looked
at her, his heart began to melt
within him and he loved the white
maiden with a raging love that
kindled a mighty fire in his bosom.

He never had been used to comb
his hair and his locks had become
stiff for want of brushing. As
soon as he saw Galatea, he began
to think how he might make himself beautiful. So he took a great
rake and raked out his hair which
hung in masses over his brows.

And he cut his shaggy beard
with a sickle and having no mirror,
he looked into the waters at his
fierce face to see how to compose

his features, how to wreathe his face in sweet smiles.

The old Cyclops had looked cross so long that it was not easy to look pleasant at once. For a long time the ships came and went in safety before him. He threw no stones at them lest the white water-nymph might see him and fear him. There is a great hill in the form of a wedge, which projects out over the sea. The waves of the ocean flow around it on both sides.

The giant sat down on the middle of this rock to watch for Galatea. He forgot his woolly sheep, which followed him because there was no one to care for them. He laid down his staff at his feet.

It was a pine-tree as large as the mast of a ship. He took up a pipe of a hundred reeds and began playing on it. So loud was his music that the mountain trembled and the sea shook from shore to shore. He sang these words playing on the pipe:

"O Galatea! fairer than the petal of the snow-white blossom, more blooming than the meadows, brighter than glass, clearer than ice, more beauteous than apples, whither has thou fled?

If thou didst know me thou wouldst repine at having fled and thou wouldst call me to thee.

I have a cave in the mountain where the warm sun is not felt in summer nor the cold in winter. There are apple-trees laden with fruit and golden grapes on the vines, as well as purple ones. I will give thee both kinds, and with thy white hands thou shalt gather strawberries in the wood-land shade.

And when I am thy husband I will

HOMER.

bring thee chestnuts and fruit from all the trees. I am so rich in cattle that I cannot count them, and here is an abundance of milk and cheese. I will give thee rab-

it covers my shoulders. Do not think it unhandsome that I am covered with stiff bristles.

A tree is covered with leaves, feathers cover the birds, and wool is an ornament to sheep. So my shaggy hair and rough beard are ornaments to me.

I have but one eye in the middle of my forehead. The Sun looks down

NEPTUNE.

from the heavens and beholds all things, yet the Sun has but one eye. And my father, Neptune, owns the sea in which you live. Him I offer you for a father-in-law.

caves. And Galatea was frightened, too, and she came swimming up to meet him, hand in hand with her hundred sisters, her face whiter than it had ever been before.

When Cyclops saw Acis hurrying to meet Galatea, the raging fire in his bosom burned more fiercely than ever and he hurled an immense rock at the youth. The rock was so large that Acis was completely buried under it and the Cyclops thought he had crushed him to death.

But Acis was instantly changed into a leaping river which ran out from under the rock and in that form went leaping toward the sea. At first it was very red, all stained with his blood, but it cleared itself as it ran on and on, growing whiter and brighter until it leapt into the sea and clasped the beautiful Galatea in its limpid eddies. Then Galatea and her hundred sisters took Acis down to their home in the sea caves and there they all lived as happily as if Cyclops had never thrown any rocks.

And now you may tell me whether we have been reading about a giant and his sheep and sea-nymphs and a gentle youth, or about a mountain, a volcano, a river, fleecy clouds, sea-waves, and other things in nature.

Spelling.

fiery   receives   frolicking   dolphins
giant   strawberries abundance   eddies

Gal a te′ a   Ne′ reus (ūse)   A′ cis

Topics for discussion.

The poetic statement of scientific facts or nature-
truths as found in this story. The poet, Ovid, as an
observer of things in nature. The perception of the
poet. The Volcano. Its cause. Resemblance to
Cyclops. The "one eye." The moaning of the
earth close to a volcano. Why Cyclops throws
stones. The raging fire in his breast. Comparison
between Cyclops cutting his shaggy beard with a
sickle and the fiery stream of lava that sweeps
forests down the sides of the volcano. The sheep
and the fleecy clouds. Acis and his "red blood."
The Red River of Arkansas. Why rivers are red.
Erosion. Why Galatea was "white." The hundred
sisters. The Cyclamen. Connection of the flower
with the myth. How myths originate.

(See Ruskin's "Queen of the Air.")

Note.

The Cyclops stories do not belong to Sicily and Ovid alone. They
are used by Homer and other writers. But this is more closely connected
with Ætna than with any other locality. Study Sicily from the map.
(See Homer's "Odyssey" and Euripides' drama "The Cyclops.")

LESSON XII.

THE OLD MAN WHO LIVED AT THE BOTTOM OF THE SEA.

IF you and I lived at the bottom of the sea, I think we should know many secrets that we never shall know, wonderful things that we can only guess at now. Did anybody ever live at the bottom of the sea? I do not believe any one ever did, but a great many stories are told about one "Old Man of the Sea" who was very mysterious and knew all the secrets that are covered up by the waters.

It is strange how many secrets we can find out from a little glass of water when we look right through it. Even in a *drop* of water we have seen under a microscope little living creatures go about like men wheeling wheelbarrows. It is no wonder then, if there has been a time when the great Sea seemed to be full of large secrets, and when some great old man living down at the bottom came up once in awhile and told them.

You know that when water freezes in a pail the ice is just the shape of the pail, and when it freezes in a pitcher it is just the shape of a pitcher. We know that water takes the shape of any dish into which it is put. And if we stand down by the sea-shore on a

stormy day, we see the water rushing into all kinds of shapes and
struggling with everything that
stands in its way, or that tries to
hold it. And then it slips away
and takes some other shape.

I wonder how it would seem to
take all kinds of shapes and never
be twice alike. Perhaps when we
came to our senses we might tell a
story more marvelous than that
which the people told in the olden
times about the "Old Man of the
Sea." I don't believe they were
talking about a man at all, but you
may not agree with me when you
hear the story.

There was a young man whose
father had gone off to the Trojan

War, but he did not come back when the war was over. The young man sailed off in a ship to find his father and he came to the country of a good king who had been in the war. The young man begged the king to tell him where his father was, so the king said, "When I came home from the war, I was kept in a strange land for a long time, because I had not remembered to pay to the gods the sacrifices due them. But a goddess pitied me and she told me that her father was the Ancient of the Deep. She was too respectful, I presume, to call him the 'Old Man of the Sea,' but it means just the same. She told me that this land was one of the places her father loved to visit when he came up from his home at the bottom of the waters.

I asked the goddess how I might snare and hold the aged deity, and she made this answer: 'When the sun has climbed into the middle of the heavens, you will see the Ancient of the Deep coming up in the form of a large wave covered with scum. Then he will take the form of a god and walk out of the waves and go into a great cave where he will lie down. There the sea-calves, the children of the Sea-side, lie down and slumber near him as they come up out of the great ocean.

They are many in number and they have a bitter smell like the salt-water of the sea. At the break of day, I will go with you, oh brave king, and show you where you will find them. But now let me tell you the strange tricks of this good old prophet. He will awake after a little while and count all the sea-calves, he will count them five at a time. And when they are numbered, he will lie down to sleep among them as a shepherd lies down among his sheep.

When you see him stretched out at length, catch him and hold him with all your strength, for he will struggle to escape. He will take

all kinds of shapes, the form of
every reptile, and every other
animal on earth, and then he will
turn into water again, and into a
raging fire. But hold him fast
and put tight bands around him.
When at last he takes the form of
an old man, let him go free, for he
will not try any longer to get away
from you. Then ask him whatever
you please and he will tell you.'

When the goddess had said this
to me, she sprang into the billowy
ocean and I went back to my ship.
When morning came, the goddess
came back and brought us each the
skin of a sea-calf that had just
been killed and wrapped us in them
so that we looked exactly like

sea-calves ourselves. Then she scooped out beds for us in the sea-sand and sat down to wait his coming. But our hiding-places sickened us, for those sea creatures have vile and bitter odors. We could hardly breathe, so the goddess brought some sweet smelling ambrosia and put it just under our noses.

We lay very quiet, and before noon the sea-calves came in a great crowd and laid themselves in rows along the shore. When the sun was at its highest, the 'Old Man of the Sea' came up out of the waves from his home at the bottom of the sea and counted all the sea-calves. He counted us with the rest and did not discover the fraud. When he had lain down to rest, we rushed out with shouts and caught him in our arms.

He did not forget his tricks but began taking all kinds of shapes, the form of a lion, a serpent, a panther, a huge boar, then he turned to water, and then he became a tall tree full of leaves. We did not let him go, however, and when he was tired out with his struggles to escape, he said, 'Oh, king, who hath taught you to take me in this snare?' I answered him, 'Old Prophet, tell me why I am kept so long in this land, away from my home, and tell me also where are the heroes who fought

with me in the Trojan War.'
Then he told me all the mysteries
I desired to know, why I was
detained, and the fates of the
heroes, and he said that your
father, whom you are seeking, my
young friend, had met with many
misfortunes and that he had lost
his ships and could not leave the
enchanted island where he was
detained. When the Old Man of
the Sea had told me these things,
he plunged into the sea and went
to his own home at the bottom of
the waters."

When the king had finished
his story, the young man went
back to his ship and sailed to
his home, thinking all the time

how best he might rescue his father.

And now you may tell me if you have ever seen the "Old Man of the Sea" come up from the great Ocean, and why he comes at noon, and what the sea-calves are, and why he is said to know so many secrets.

Spelling.

mysterious   pitied   deity   nectar
microscope   ancient   reptile   ambrosia

Pro teus (tūse)

Topics for discussion.

Forms of water. The reason why water takes so many forms. Salt-water. Why the ocean is salty. The tides. The tides at noon. The idea of Proteus or the "Old Man of the Sea" as connected with the tides.

(See Homer's "Odyssey" for the original of this story, and Hawthorne's "Wonder Book" for a fine version of it.)

LESSON XIII.

WHAT HAPPENED WHEN THE SUN FORGOT TO BEHAVE WELL.

IT is evidently the duty of the Sun as he goes round and round the earth to distribute his favors equally on all. It does not look well for such a great creature, who carries all the sunshine and has the power of making everybody happy or miserable, to shine smilingly on one person or on one blossom and neglect another. How could the violet grow if all the sunshine were given to the rose? How could the rose blush if the Sun should forget all about her and shine only on the buttercup? No indeed, it does not look well in people in high office to have favorites, and shower all the smiles upon them and keep all the frowns for other people. When the Sun took it upon himself to distribute sunshine to all the world, he should have started out with the determination to be just as good to one person as to another. And he should have made up his mind to keep the days and nights of equal length.

But it is said of him that he

looked down upon the Ocean and saw a pretty creature, very white and very gentle, something which you and I would call an ocean wave. The Sun did not call it a wave. He said it was the "White Lady of the Sea," and he gazed and gazed at her and forgot to go around the earth for days at a time. This made some parts of the earth very cold, those parts of it which could not get the least glimpse of him, and the flowers in those places, as well as the people, almost froze to death. They couldn't grow and they wondered why the Sun did not come around and give them daylight and warm them up with sunshine.

When the Sun had gazed a long time at the "White Lady of the Sea," he would suddenly remember that he ought to be going around the earth and he would start on, running as fast as he could go, so that he would get around too soon, and that made the days very short, too short in fact, sometimes.

And again, when he came over the ocean and saw the pretty wave, he would linger and gaze at her, and wish she would take his hand and go round the earth with him, until even in mid-winter when the days were expected to be shortest, they became altogether too long. You would not believe me if I should tell you how the Sun behaved. Sometimes he was so troubled that a great dark shadow came over his face, and the birds and flowers and people were all alarmed. You and I call it an eclipse, but the flowers did not call it that. They said he was in grief because the Moon had got in the way so that he could not look at the "White Lady of the Sea."

The pretty white wave did not notice the Sun very much, however. She did not know that people and flowers were deprived of sunshine on her account. She was a happy princess, daughter of the kingly Ocean.

There were many other white waves, her beautiful handmaidens

who served her, and they all
used to sit near the door of her
father's palace spinning and weaving. They wove sashes of sea-foam,
and sailors have often saved themselves from drowning by wearing
these girdles. When the Sun
found out that the "White Lady of
the Sea" did not even notice him,
he said, "I will change myself into
a great white wave which shall
look just like her mother. And I
will go and speak to her and then
she will notice me."

So the Sun put away his golden
chariot and turned his horses into
a pasture away off in the West,
where they could feed upon ambrosia to their hearts' content, for

the horses of the gods do not eat grass. Then the Sun plunged into the Ocean and took on the likeness of a great brilliant wave. You ought to have seen it as it went rolling along toward the White Lady of the Sea. The Sun entered the door of the palace where the White Lady sat spinning and, kissing her dainty forehead, took his own form again and told her that he was the god who measured out the year, who beheld all things, and gave light to all the world. When the White Lady of the Sea saw the great shining Sun so near her, she was frightened and threw down her spindle.

Now there was a fair nymph who

lived in the fields, who was troubled because the sunlight did not come to her every day and she sought to find the reason for the Sun's delay. When the days were short she grew pale from the cold and darkness and shuddered for fear when he did not come out at all. She watched and watched, until she discovered that the Sun wasted his time in gazing after the White Lady of the Sea; and when she saw him actually kissing her she sent word about it to her father, Old Ocean.

Old Ocean called to his daughter and told her to hurry away to the land, and he sent a wave to hasten her flight. So she ran to the shore and as she hurried up onto the sand she sank down into it and never was seen again. Then the Sun sent his beams to search for her down among the grains of sand, and he sprinkled the earth into which she sank with sweet-smelling nectar, and said, " Still shalt thou reach the skies as incense."

So there grew up a frankincense-tree in the place where the beautiful White Lady was lost. But the Sun refused to shine any more on the pretty nymph that lived in the field. There she sat on the bare ground with her hair in frightful disorder and flying in every direction. For nine days she lived on dew and tears, without food or water. She did not raise herself from the ground

but turned her face in the direction
of the Sun as he moved along, pray-
ing for a little sunshine.

The Sun would not look at her,
however, and when she tried to
rise from the ground, they say that
her feet had taken root so that she
was held fast, and that she had
changed into a sun-flower and that
she could do nothing else but turn
around on her stem and look at the
Sun.

I knew a boy who said that the
sun-flower never turned around to
look at the sun, and so his sister
used to go out every morning and
turn them toward the east and at
night she would turn them to the
west; but he found out her joke.

I believe this story is true — that is — a part of it, because I have seen a whole row of sun-flowers hang their heads over a fence to look at the sun, and I have seen other flowers stretch their necks a long way to try to get a little sunshine.

Spelling.

miserable	determination	couldn't
chariot	smilingly	glimpse
eclipse	frankincense	

Topics for discussion.

The action of sunlight. Necessity of sunlight to growth. This story of Clytie is a myth from Ovid. Let the pupils interpret it. W. D. Howell's story "The Pumpkin-Glory" is a similar illustration of the action of plants in reaching for the light.

The eclipse. Eclipse of the sun, — moon.

Action of water running upon the sand.

(See John Burrough's essay "A Sea Breeze.")

LESSON XIV.

A TALE WITH TWO HEROES.

APOLLO.

THERE is a beautiful lake in the West in the shape of a big foot. Its banks are gay with wild flowers and its shores are lined with pebbles. Hills covered with great forests of oak and maple surround the lake, and large fishes sport in its waters. There is a little river running out of it, and there are many springs rising up into it from the sandy bed below.

There used to be a little pond down at one side of the toe of this big water foot, in which there were a great many kinds of living creatures at different seasons of the year, but they all died a peculiar death at last.

This is how the pond came. There were seasons when the lake was very high. It could not contain all the water that came into it and the little outlet could not carry off the extra water fast enough. Then the lake overflowed its banks and the waters ran into a hollow near by and there was the pond.

At first the pond was full of bright, clear water, and people left their row-boats in " the bay," as they called it. They said the boats were safe there, because they could not be carried by the winds out into the lake.

A little boy whose name was Max, lived in an old-fashioned house down by the lake. The pond was right in front of the house, and he loved to play in the boats or dig in the mud on the banks. He made little ships and sailed them on the pond, and he picked up flat stones from the lake shore and threw them across the pond. When the stones touched the water, they would glance up and fly along through the air and then touch the water again. Max called this making the stones skip.

When there were long hot seasons, the water began to dry out of the pond, and sometimes it was so dry that Max could almost walk across it. Bulrushes, cat-tails, reeds, and yellow water-lilies grew in the mud, and wild iris. Sometimes the pond was perfectly purple with wild iris. Snakes, lizards, snails, and worms crawled in its slimy bed, and toads hopped all around its shores. You ought to have seen the army of tiny little toads that sometimes came out into the road.

You would have thought that there was a crusade in the toad

family.   Max thought that they
were very cunning.   After a shower
he used to see hundreds of them.
Angle worms crawled up out of the
mud by the thousand, and Max
wondered where they came from.
He asked some other boys about it
and they said the angle worms
dropped down out of the sky, and
Max believed it for awhile.   Frogs
lived in the pond, and croaked and
sang very loudly at night when
Max went to bed.

Max did not sleep very well, and
he often lay awake and listened to
them.   He used to wake in the
night, and he would get up and sit
by the window and look out upon
the pond.   He often saw a great

white cloud standing over it. It was a misty vapor coming up from the pond. Beyond it was a forest where a lonesome whip-poor-will sang, and Max imagined the mist to be a great giantess in a white robe, and the call of the bird to be the song of the giantess.

After awhile Max's father thought the pond was a bad thing to exist so close to a town, for many children were sick with a terrible fever. So he took his wagon and his shovel and started out for a hill where the roads were bad. And he hauled a great deal of dirt down to the pond and threw it in until there was not any pond left, but there was a little park instead.

And he smoothed down the bad road at the same time, so that he left a good one in its place, and he never asked any one to think about it or remember it. Indeed, he never once thought himself a hero, and did not expect any thanks. If any one had praised him, he would have been greatly astonished.

In the olden times, there was another pond; it was at the foot of a high mountain, and the mists which rose out of it were poisonous, so that the people living near had dreadful fevers. There was no one to fill up the pond with dirt, but the sun came out and shone very brightly, and drove the vapors away, and after awhile there was a story about it which all the people told each other, and they believed it. This is the story:

Old Earth was the mother of everything. She was the mother of all the animals, and of seeds which grow up into beautiful shapes. When rivers and lakes which overflowed their banks went back to their beds, the people found all sorts of living creatures under the stones, and in the mud. "So it must be that the earth is the mother of them," they said.

There was one great creature, the Python, which was like a serpent, and it rose from the earth very early and went out to destroy men. So ravenous and greedy was it, that it devoured multitudes.

People grew sick and died from its terrible breath; and they fled before it for a long time. At last, however, there came a great hero who carried a golden bow with golden arrows. He had never before shot at anything but timid animals, like the goat or deer or rabbit. But now he aimed a thousand arrows at the serpent.

The snake grew weaker and weaker from his many wounds, and died. Then the people rejoiced, and the hero, for fear his deed would be forgotten, gave commands that there should be festivals held in his honor, called the Pythian games, at which the men and boys should run races and sing songs.

The prize for the victor was a wreath of laurel, and he also received a palm-branch. In this way this hero was remembered eight hundred years, but the one who turned the pond into a park was forgotten in less than a week.

I wonder which you think was the greater hero, the man who filled the pond by hard labor, digging and carrying dirt, or the god which shot the golden arrows at the serpent. And I wonder whether old Python is ever seen nowadays, and if he still destroys men with his poisonous breath.

Spelling.

peculiar   hauled   giantess   devoured
poisonous   iris   croaked   Python

Topics for discussion.

The greater hero. Nobility of labor. Bravery
compared with courage. Daring to do hard things.
Why Millet paints pictures of laboring people as
being more beautiful than pictures of fashionable
people. Self-respect better than the respect of others.
Humility better than fame. Was there really a
Python. Interpretation of the Myth. Other stories
that make mists to be unearthly creatures. (Beowulf.
Erl-King.) Why the ancients made myths. The
truth in myths. The poetic form of the myth.
Relation of sunlight to health. Angle-worms —
where they come from. Toads — their habits and
homes. Frogs. Study of tadpoles.

Note.

The story of the Python is told by Hesiod and by Ovid.

LESSON XV.

HOW A LITTLE HERO CONQUERED A LARGE ONE.

THERE was once a tall lady who wore long dark, trailing robes, so long and so dark that it made the whole world seem like night. The birds went to sleep when they saw her coming, and the stars came out to shine as her long black robe swept over the land. Her name was Leto, (Darkness,) and she wandered round and round the earth twenty-four hours out of the night, for, as we have said, it was never day-time where she was.

At last she grew tired, and thought she would like to stop

awhile, and she sought for a place
to rest. She kept on seeking for
such a spot until she came to an
island, called Delos, and she said if
she could find a home there that
the place should become glorious.
It should be the birth-place of
Apollo who would be a great hero.
A large white temple should be
built in his honor, and wise men
should come from every part of the
earth to lay rich gifts on his altar.

So the good people of the island
made a home for her, and there
Apollo was born, and at his birth
the whole earth laughed and grew
gay with flowers. Before that,
Delos had been only a stony island,
and of no particular account, but

now it was called the bright-land, and it was girt around by a golden wall, and its lakes and rivers all turned into gold and shone like the sun.

There were seven snowy swans that left their home in a golden river and went to circle around his cradle and sing sweet songs to his mother. They were the birds of the Muses, and took him the gift of song, so that he should be a musician.

And that was not all. The island became golden to its foundations, and the olive trees took on golden foliage, and the rivers ran over with gold. The child could not tell a lie, which was another golden circumstance, and he had a golden harp with golden strings.

There came beautiful nymphs who wrapped him in white robes embroidered with gold, that looked just like the white clouds of early morning fringed with gold when the sun is just rising. You may think this is a pretty large story, and you may doubt it, but if you take a sail some day around the island of Delos just as the sun is rising, you will see that it is all quite true.

As soon as the babe could breathe a little, the goddess of Justice fed him with nectar and ambrosia, and then he took his harp with the golden strings and began to play sweet tunes and sing songs, and to lay down the law like any other baby. While yet a child, Apollo wore a belt of gold about his waist, but it turned into a golden sword, and he carried a quiver filled with golden arrows which never missed the mark any more than a sunbeam does when it strikes at a boy's face to give him little golden freckles.

Before Apollo was an hour old he became a famous traveller. Like his mother, he travelled all the time, going round and round the earth twenty-four hours out of the day, for it was never night-time where he was. He saw all the lands on the face of the earth, and

after awhile he thought it would be
pleasant to settle down and have a
home somewhere, at least for one
whole day, and he came to a
Fountain that was so beautiful that
he thought he would make his
home near her. But the pretty
Fountain did not like his attentions.
He was too bright, and she feared
that he would send his arrows at
her, so she begged him to go on,
for fear that they might cease to
like each other.

Apollo went on until he came to
a mountain where wise people
loved to linger. It was called
Mont Parnassus; and there he built
himself a shrine, and he kindled an
undying fire on his altar as large

and as red as the setting sun, and he taught the people how to worship him.

He charged them to tell the truth always, and to be kind to all who came with gifts to his temple. There he slew a great serpent called Python, a monster of darkness and pestilence, which kept the people away from his temple. This monster arose from the wet earth, and it was a source of terror to all the people living near the mountain.

Apollo had never before shot such dreadful beasts, but he sent a thousand arrows at him, and the poisonous serpent died of his wounds. To keep the fame of this deed in the minds of men, Apollo commanded that there should be games, in which young men should run races, and the conqueror should have a crown of leaves from the beech tree.

Apollo was so proud of this victory, and said so much about it, that a little fellow with wings whose name was Cupid, grew angry with him. He carried a bow, as well as Apollo, and a quiver full of arrows, and he claimed to be a more skillful sharpshooter than the god of the golden bow. Then Cupid said to Apollo, "Your bow may shoot all things on earth, but my bow shall shoot you, and your glory shall be less than mine."

People are very small, you know, when they are more anxious for the glory than for the pleasure that there is in doing something good.

So Cupid flew through the air with beating wings and a beating heart, and stood upon the top of the mountain. And he drew two arrows from his quiver, one to breed hatred, — that arrow was made of lead, — and one to breed love, which was made of gold.

The arrow of lead was blunt, and the golden arrow very sharp. Cupid shot the golden arrow at Apollo, but with the blunt arrow of lead he pierced the heart of a beautiful maiden. At once Apollo loved the girl and she hated him. He tried to catch her but she fled. Apollo called out to her and this is what he said: "O beautiful maiden, stop I pray you. I am not your enemy. You fly from me as a lamb flies from a wolf, or as a deer flies from a lion. It is because I love you that I follow you. I am not a rude, coarse man. I am not a shepherd. I am very rich in gold and cattle, and I have built great cities. I make beautiful music on the harp, and I can see all things present and future, and I prepare medicines. Cupid's arrow has wounded my heart, but I cannot make the medicine to cure that. If you will come with me I will make you my wife."

But the girl fled faster than ever, and at last she hid in a laurel bush close to a river, and the river-god, who was her father, caused the bushes to grow around her so quickly that she seemed to turn into a tree.

If we believe the story, her body was covered with a thin bark, her hair grew into green leaves, her arms into branches, and her feet became the roots to hold her into the ground.

Nothing remained to her but her elegance, but that was quite enough for Apollo, and so he threw his arms around her and kissed her bark and exclaimed, "Since I cannot win you for a wife, you shall be my tree. My golden hair and my harp shall always be adorned by your leaves."

Thus was the great hero conquered by the little one, but to this day poets and singers wear a crown of laurel.

Spelling.

Parnassus	foliage	pestilence
laurel	glorious	embroidered
conqueror	trailing	

Note to Teachers.

This story, which is gleaned from Callimachus 300 B.C., Ovid 19 B.C., and other classic writers, is doubtless a "Solar Myth" or sun story. Leto or darkness is the mother of daylight and so on. There are many other stories connected with the Island of Delos and Mount Parnassus which the pupils ought to know. (See Dr. Schlieman's "Excavations at Troy," "Murray's Mythology," Cox's "Manual of Mythology," and Gayley's "Classic Myths in English Literature.")

Topics for discussion.

The practice of crowning poets, statesmen, kings, etc. The artist's point of view, golden effects of sunlight. What is true in the story. What is only poetic fancy. What is real history. Why the Sun is a "god of medicine." Why the Sun is an archer. What is his golden sword? Why he is a seer. A prophet. Why does Apollo "never tell a lie"? Daphne (the dawn) flies from him. When? When does she "hide in shrubs"?

What is going on in Greece now near the shrine of Apollo? See accounts of the excavations at Delphi, Delos, Daphne, Argos, and Athens.

LESSON XVI.

AN OLD STORY FROM TADPOLE LAND.

You tell me that Tadpole Land is down in a ditch near your own house, and you say that tadpoles are hatched from eggs, and that they have tails and plumes which they get rid of as they grow older and more frisky. Then they become frogs and begin to multiply their legs by two, and they jump and croak. Either you have not used your eyes well, or else people saw differently in the olden times, for they told quite another story.

There was once, ages and ages ago, a beautiful woman, and she was tall and very quiet. She wore dark purple robes or black ones, and they were so long that they trailed behind her for miles.

She travelled all the time going round the earth in one direction, always toward the west.

Her long robes were very light and airy. She went right along over rivers and lakes and bushes, but her trailing garments never seemed to catch on the bushes, or get soiled in the dust and mud, or wet in ponds and rivers.

Very remarkable robes were those, and I am sure that it would gratify the fine ladies of later days if they could find some of the same sort but with longer trains perhaps.

This beautiful woman was called Leto in some lands, and Latona in others. She carried two very pretty babes in her arms, and she wrapped her black veil around them so that no one could see them, for one was as bright as the sky before sunrise, and the other was as bright as the sky after sunset, and it would have been almost like daylight if they had not been hidden under the veil.

After Latona had wandered around the earth for many years, she became very weary and thirsty, for many of the fields over which she passed were scorched by the heat of summer. After awhile she came to the banks of a lake and sat down on its shore. She dipped her hand in the water and began to drink from it.

There were some rude country men down at the lake gathering willows to make baskets, and they forbade her to drink. They tried to scare her away but she said to them, "Why do you deny me a drink of water? Water was made for all to drink, and I beg of you to let me be."

But they laughed at her, and were ruder than before, so she showed them the two little babes, hoping that they might have pity on her.

The rough fellows only used abusive language and threw stones

into the water to make it muddy
so that she could not drink it.
Then Latona raised her hands to
heaven, and uttered a prayer that
the wicked men might always live
in the mud.

She went on her way, and as
she looked back she saw the men
jumping up and down in the mud.
They began to grow smaller and
smaller, and the last she saw and
heard of them, they had become
frogs, and had to keep on calling
out the same ugly words they had
said to her, in the same harsh
voices. And there they are to this
day croaking and leaping.

Perhaps this story is true and
perhaps it is not, but the easiest

way for you to find out is to watch the tadpole from the time it is an egg until it croaks.

And you might also watch that greedy animal who will never give any one even a drink of water, and who calls names and says ugly words, and then you will know whether he really lives in the mud or whether he carries the mud in his heart.

Spelling.

La to' na   frisky   croak   differently
airy   gratify   veil   forbade

Topics for discussion.

The development of the frog.

Interpretation of the myth. The truth in it. The moral point.

Dante makes punishment to consist in the continuance of a bad action. "He who wrongs another wrongs himself, because he makes himself bad." Marcus Aurelius.

LESSON XVII.

A STORY OF THE SETTING SUN.

THERE were three goddesses who lived in the garden of Hesperides where the golden apples grow. They were very beautiful and rosy, with white robes and golden hair. They guarded the golden apples and watched over their favorite brother, Phaeton, whose father was the great, shining sun-god Apollo.

Apollo used to drive the chariot of the Sun, and he was very skillful and wise about it. He kept it right in the middle of the heavens where it never ran against anything.

But Phaeton had heard some one say that he did not believe he was the son of Apollo, because he never drove the heavenly horses and was not allowed the honors of a royal prince. Phaeton begged his father, therefore, to let him drive the horses and guide the chariot just for one day, so that he should prove to the people who sneered at him that he really was beloved of Apollo, and his true son. The father unwillingly consented, and

Phaeton mounted the chariot and drove off at great speed, but he was unskillful, and the horses ran hither and thither in confusion, and soon the unhappy youth had driven so close to the earth that he had scorched its surface everywhere, set the rivers all boiling, dried up the fountains, burned the trees and the grass, and killed many people.

Jupiter in his wrath, seeing all these things, sent a thunderbolt to strike him dead, and his beautiful sisters mourned and wept over him. They took his body to a field beyond the garden of Hesperides and buried it, and erected over it a marble tomb on which was inscribed these words, "Here lies

Phaeton, the driver of his father's chariot, which he failed to manage. He died in the attempt to do a great thing." His father, Apollo, sorrowed greatly over the loss of his son. If we can believe what they say, he passed a whole day in sorrow, covering his face, and he did not drive the chariot through the heavens for that day, so that the earth was left in darkness. The flaming forests set on fire by Phaeton furnished all the light there was.

The mother of Phaeton, whose name was Clymene, was a tall, dark-robed goddess, whose abode was beneath the earth. When she learned of the fate of her beloved son, she traversed the whole earth, going round and round it full of woe, seeking his lifeless form, and at last she came to a stream in the field beyond the garden of Hesperides, on whose bank was the tomb of Phaeton. She laid herself down on the spot and bathed the stone with her tears and warmed it with her kisses. The daughters of the Sun mourned no less and wept unavailing tears over his death. There they called upon him night and day, and lay on the ground near his tomb.

Four times did the Moon fill out her great round disk while they remained at the tomb and uttered lamentations. Jupiter was angry with them for mourning so long over their brother, and decreed that they should remain at the tomb and continue weeping forever. When they tried to rise from the ground they found that their feet were rooted to the spot, and that their arms were stiffened. They had turned into weeping-willow trees.

When their mother saw them turning into trees, she ran to them and pressed her lips to theirs in a last kiss, and the bark of the tree came over them and covered them. There they continued standing, and the tears oozed down their new formed branches and hardened in the sun. The rain beat upon them and carried the hardened tears off into the river, down to the sea, and the sailors gathered them for jewels. But Jupiter said to the other gods, let no one dare to condemn the will of Zeus. Behold the fate of these maidens. Their fidelity has been their ruin.

Spelling.

Hesperides	fidelity	stiffened
lamentations	oozed	confusion

Topics for discussion.

The main point of the story. Fidelity. Did the sisters deserve their punishment? Excessive grief.

Origin of amber, the tears which " sailors gather as jewels."

(See Jane Andrews's story of the "Amber Beads.")

LESSON XVIII.

WHY THE SWAN LOVES THE WATER.

HAVE you ever been to the parks and watched the swans floating about on the water? If you have, perhaps you have seen them come up on the land, and have noticed how red their toes are and how wide the web is between the toes, making good paddles of their feet when they are in the water. Their feathers are white and glossy, and their bill is broad and flat without any point. I have heard that they sing a sweet song just as they are about to die, but that may be a fancy. There is a pretty story told about the swan, which reads as follows:

There was a young prince named Phaeton, with long yellow hair, whose father drove the chariot of the Sun. Phaeton begged his father to let him drive for one day only, and the god of the Sun unwillingly gave his consent. Phaeton mounted the chariot, but not being a skillful driver, he drove too near the earth, and set it on fire, and the rivers all began to boil. So Jupiter, who had charge of the whole world, sent a thunderbolt to slay the young prince. Phaeton had a friend who was a noble man as well as a great king, and whose name was Cycnus.

Cycnus loved Phaeton very much, and when he heard of his sad end, he left his kingdom and all of his people and went out into a forest where he wept aloud, mourning and complaining because his friend was lost to him. He wept until his voice became shrill, crying aloud, calling the name of the lost one. His hair turned white and became like feathers, but he wept on and on. At last his neck became very long, and he found himself all clothed in white feathers. A bill without a point grew upon his lips, and soft membranes joined his toes, and he had become a new bird.

But he would never trust himself

to fly, for he had seen fire come from the air when it struck his beloved Phaeton. He chose to remain in the pools and in wide lakes, where he might be safe from fire. There he lives to this day, a beautiful swan, swimming about in the clear waters, mourning for his lost friend.

And I am sure we respect him more with his flat bill and the webs between his toes, than a king on his throne who cannot remember his friend any longer than it suits his fancy. And we would rather sit on a cold lake all day with our hearts sincere and true, than to sit on a throne with no love in our hearts for loyalty.

Spelling.

glossy	sincere	feathers
chariot	Pha´e ton	Cyc´ nus
membranes	noticed	

Topics for discussion.

Water-birds, waders, swimmers.
Why one has long legs and the other short legs.
Broad bills — why.   Web-toes.
Interpretation of the myth as a nature story.

LESSON XIX.

HOW CORONIS BECAME A CROW.

It has been the impression in times past, that people sprang from the earth. That the sun shining on the earth or the rain falling there, in some mysterious way caused races of people to spring up. I suppose that is because there are so many things which do spring from the earth in unaccountable ways. Old king Cecrops was a hero so ancient, that all we know of him is, that he was said to have sprung from the earth in the form of a snake, and that a high hill (the Acropolis) is named after him; and, further, it was during his reign that Poseidon and Athena contested the naming of Athens, which before that had been called Cecropia. Cecrops had three daughters, whose names all showed that they were really drops of dew. Whenever it is very warm and the ground is moist, great numbers of snakes and worms are found, and there is apt to be dew-drops every morning.

After Cecrops died, there came another king. He was a huge snake and sprang from the ground. The Earth was said to be his mother, and the God of Fire his father, and he might have died only that the Goddess of Wisdom, Athena, saved him. She wove a basket of twigs and bulrushes, (perhaps you can go to a swamp and find such a basket,) and concealed the snake-like baby in it, and gave it to the three maidens, the dew-drops by name and nature, to care for, and she told them not to pry into its secrets but to keep the basket closed.

Another maiden whose name was Coronis, was hiding in the bushes when the dew-maidens took the basket. Coronis was a very bright creature. Her face shone like a golden sunbeam, and she seemed to be crowned with light. Coronis was beloved of the goddess Athena, and she served her whenever she could. So she stood in the hiding-place and watched the three maidens who had the basket to see what they would do. She suspected that they would be too curious to keep the basket closed.

Sure enough they peeped in, at least two of them did, and when they saw the snaky child they were so frightened that they ran and threw themselves into the sea. Now the dewy maidens and the sea are mysteriously related, and the ocean god was very angry when he found that his relatives were watched by Coronis. He found out, too, that she had gone to Athena and told that goddess that the maidens had opened the basket.

So he pretended to love Coronis, and he begged her to throw herself into the water that he might carry her about in his great arms, and give her a beautiful home. But Coronis was afraid of him and fled, and he rose in anger and pursued her with his great waves, hoping to drown her in the boiling waters. Coronis ran as fast as she could, but he had almost captured her, when she threw up her arms in a beseeching manner to the Goddess of Wisdom and begged to be saved.

Athena, seeing her danger, looked with mercy upon her. The arms of Coronis began to be covered with feathers. Her garments became black and took root in her flesh.

She was lifted up from the ground and began to fly into the heavens, and was seated on Athena's right hand. She had become a crow, and there she sat and chattered to her heart's content. Her punishment is that she must always tell tales and be black.

Spelling.

impression	unaccountable	suspected
pursued	mysterious	ancient

Po'sei (sī) don, the god of the water. Another name for him was Neptune. Athena,—the same as the Roman Minerva. Co ro'nis, a crown.

Topics for discussion.

The Acropolis at Athens. All Greek cities had an Acropolis or "highest point." The Acropolis is the most noted hill in the world, and it is well worth any teacher's time in the lowest primary grades to study models and pictures of it, and tell the stories connected with it to the children. Mars Hill is just at the foot of it. There are numberless stories of Athena, the Goddess of Wisdom, connected with it. The Parthenon standing on the Acropolis is the most famous of all ruins.

Moral point of the myth. Tale-bearers.

Curiosity.

The myth as a Nature Story.

How the dew "runs to the sea."

Coronis (or sunlight) seeing into the secrets of nature.

Note.

For the original see Ovid's Metamorphoses.

LESSON XX.

THE EVIL THAT CAME OF NOT LOVING NATURE.

PEOPLE used to say that there was a god of nature. They loved trees, and flowers, and rivers, and all the creatures that live out of doors. They thought these things were worth studying, and that there were gods all about them who lived among these open air things and protected them. Sometimes we think that there is no wisdom except in books, and we make bats of ourselves, shutting ourselves up in dark houses, instead of finding the wisdom that there is in the flowers and trees and sunshine. There was one of the nature gods who loved the grape-vine, and I am sorry to say that he liked the juice better than the grape. People used to dance and sing songs in honor of this god. They even built him a temple, and worshipped him, and held festivals in his honor.

There were three young women, however, who did not honor the god. They wore dark dresses, and wove beautiful cloth in the dark-ness, and they would never go to the festivals where the god of the vine was worshipped. In fact they went right on with their work, and acted as badly as you would if you took your knitting to church.

But something strange happened to them, because they did not love the gladness and light of nature. The looms on which they wove their beautiful cloth began to put forth ivy leaves. Their threads changed into vines.

The purple cloth they were weaving turned into grapes; and when the day was past, their house seemed to shake, while torches burned all around, and glowing fires lit up every room.

Phantoms of wild beasts howled

around, and the sisters tried to hide themselves, avoiding the fires and the light. While they were seeking a hiding-place, a membrane was stretched over their small limbs, and it covered their arms with thin wings.

In the darkness they could not discover how it happened, but they lost their shape. They had no feathers to bear them up, but they supported themselves on their thin wings. Their voices became squeaking and small, and the power to love the woods was taken away from them, so that they always staid in dark corners of houses and were called bats.

Spelling.

protected juice knitting avoiding
phantom festivals membrane squeaking

Topics for discussion.

What is the interpretation of this myth? The
story sounds as if it came from what poet? The
underlying motive of the story. What people live
out of doors? Why? What people remain closely
in houses? Compare Italians and the French with
Americans and Germans in this respect.

LESSON XXI.

ROCKS, WAVES, AND SUNSHINE.

THERE is a gleam on the water on a sunny day and a long bright path when the moon comes up at night. The sea-weed shines when it is cast up wet on the shore as if it carried part of this radiance with it. We have heard of a rock out in the sea, a great bare rock over which the gleaming waves continually break.

They rush toward it and encircle it with their shining arms, and they wash the green sea-weed upon it until one might, in imagination, paint the picture of a great sea-god with a green beard and gleaming eyes endeavoring to clasp some lone water-nymph to his heart.

There was a youth who wandered on the shore near this rock. Sometimes he would drag the net up and down the shore and sweep up many fish into its meshes, or else he would spring to the rock and catch fish with a line.

There was a verdant meadow close to the shore, one part of which was surrounded with water, and the other with a kind of grass which the horned cattle would not eat nor would the sheep or goats touch it. The bees did not collect honey from it, and the mowers had never cut it. One day

when the youth had caught many
fish he sat down on the grass, and,
after putting his net to dry, laid
the fish in rows that he might
count them. Some of the fish he
had taken with the hook and they
were hurt, others he had driven
into his net and they were choked
in their struggles. As soon as the
fish touched the grass they seemed
endued with life once more. They
began to move about and shift from
side to side, and after a little they
skipped about on the land and then
they danced off into the sea and
left their new master alone on the
green meadow.

The young man was astonished,
and wondered what could be the

cause of this, — whether some divinity had done it or whether the fish had eaten some enchanted herb. "What herb," said the youth to himself, "could have such magical power?" With that he plucked some of the grass and ate it, but he had hardly swallowed it before he felt himself possessed of the nature of a different creature. He began to dance about and soon he seemed to be obliged to leap into the sea. As he leaped forth he cried out, "Farewell, oh beautiful land! I shall never visit thee again!" and he plunged under the waters.

The gods of the sea received him with honors, and they entreated

Old Ocean to wash away from him all signs of mortality. So the Ocean purified him and the gods repeated a charm over him nine times, to take away all his earthly sins, and they commanded him to dive below a hundred streams. This he did, and whole seas came pouring over his head, and he fell asleep. When he awoke he found himself in a new body entirely different from his former body, and he was not the same in mind. He had a long green beard and flowing hair which swept over his huge shoulders and floated on the waves like sea-weeds. His arms were the color of the sky above, and his body was like that of a fish. He had

become a sea-god and they called
him Glaucus, the Gleaming-Eyed.

As he swam about in the calm
sea he looked like the path of light
which you see across the lake on
a bright summer morning. And
when it stormed he let his white
sea-horses rove over the billows,
for he was the master of the steeds
of the sea.

It happened as Glaucus was
swimming about in the waters one
day that a lovely sea-nymph
wandered along the shore, and
when Glaucus saw her he rushed
toward her like a gleaming
wave hurrying toward the shore.
His green beard and his
long flowing locks floated loosely

on the waves; one might have thought that the waters had gathered up all the sea-weeds and sea-grasses for miles around.

When the nymph, whose name was Scylla, saw him coming toward her she was frightened and ran along the shore as fast as she could, hoping to escape him. And Glaucus called out to her, "Oh, beauteous maiden, I am not a monster but a sea-king. I pray thee look upon me with kindness, and if thou wilt be my bride I will give thee a red-gold throne down in the ocean palace which is my home."

But Scylla was as badly scared as ever when she heard his loud voice, so she sped along until she reached the top of a mountain, close to the shore.

In front of the sea, there is a huge ridge which ends in one bare pointed rock. This rock bends for a long distance over the sea and it has no trees upon it. Here she stood secure and looked at the god, admiring his color and his flowing hair with great wonder. Then he told her his story, but she still feared him, and she hid away from him in the dark cave in the rock.

And Glaucus flung himself up onto the rocks and tried to climb over their watery stones that he might find Scylla, but he could not hold on, the rocks were so slippery.

He swam about here and there among the crags, but he could not even glance for one moment into the cave where the nymph was hiding.

Then Glaucus thought of a sunny-faced goddess who lived on an island covered with grassy hills. She was the daughter of Sun and Ocean, and her name was Circe. By the sunshine which radiated from her own face she could light up the darkest cave and see into all of its secret corners. She lived in a palace of snow-white marble, as grand as the marble-white towers which the clouds seem to form in the sky after a rain.

Her halls were filled with wild

beasts. They loved to lie at her feet and let her caress them with her warm hand, just as the lion loves to lie down and rest in the sunshine. She knew all sorts of charms and could cause clouds to rise from the sea, and flowers to spring from the ground. She could wave her magic wand over the ripening grape and instil a charm into its juices, by which she could turn men into wild beasts.

So Glaucus stabled in the sea caves the wild white steeds which had been committed to his care, and he left the field of the Cyclops and the mountain which rests on a giant's jaws and went swimming away to find the island of Circe.

His green beard and long hair floated all about on the water, and his huge hands were spread out to pull himself over the gleaming path which the sun threw before him.

When Glaucus arrived at the island of Circe and beheld the goddess he said to her, "Oh lovely goddess, daughter of the Sun, I pray thee pity me in my trouble. I beseech thee to come to the rock and light up the cave wherein the beautiful Scylla has hidden herself. And wilt thou teach her to be friendly to the sea-waves strewn with grasses and thy servant Glaucus who must ever be lonely if she frowns upon him, for hatred is cold and hard to bear."

Then Circe, daughter of the golden Sun, cast the radiance of her face upon him and answered, "If Scylla be cold and hard like the rock and frown upon thee, do thou remain here in my kingdom. The radiance of the Sun shall be thine, and kindly smiles and warm friendship."

But Glaucus made this scornful reply, "Sooner shall foliage grow in the ocean, sooner shall sea-weed grow on the tops of mountains, than I shall cease to love Scylla. The cruel rock wherein she hides is better than thy warm halls."

The goddess was angry when she heard these words, and she put on her azure vestments, and taking

the juices of poisonous plants with
her, she stepped out into the
boiling waters. She walked with
bare feet along on the waves as
firmly as if she were walking on
dry land; wherever her feet touched
the sea rain clouds rose into the sky.

Now there was a little bay
curving in the shape of a bow
among the secret places of the
rocks where Scylla went to bathe
when the sun was highest in the
heavens. Circe found this little
bay and threw the poisoned juices
into it, saying to herself, " Since
Glaucus scorns the warmth and
sunlight of the halls of Circe, he
shall be scorned by the nymph
whom he loves."

Circe said some strange words of magic over the waters and then she departed. Hardly had she gone when Scylla, not knowing that the waters had been charmed, stepped into the bay to take a bath. No sooner had she plunged beneath the waters than she found herself changing into a horrible rock full of ugly caves, a rock as cold and hard as that which frowned down upon the sea.

And she found herself surrounded by frightful dogs, barking and biting, and when she put her hand down to drive them away she could not; they had taken up their abode in the caves and had become a part of herself. Their mouths were open and their jaws ready to devour all who came in their way, and they barked continually. And there Scylla stands now, just as she stood ages and ages ago, and the dogs are barking at Glaucus day and night.

The poisoned waters keep on working their charms, and the waters in the little bay rise and give Scylla a bath at noontide.

And now you may tell me whether there is any better way of telling about sea-weeds and sea-waves and tides, paths of light on the water, the beating of rocks by the waters to form sea-waves, and the action of the sun and his golden rays.

Spelling.

radiance	imagination	azure	Cir′ce
Glau′cus	magical	Scyl′la	biting

Topics for discussion.

Action of salt water on rocks.

Paths on the water. Sea-weeds.

Stories of Scylla as found in Homer's "Odyssey."

Note.

The rock Scylla is just off the southwestern coast of Italy, opposite Sicily. It stands boldly out into the water, and many smaller rocks are scattered about at the base. Back of the rock there appears to be a small village.

The original of this story is found in Ovid.

LESSON XXII.

DO UNTO TREES AS YOU WOULD HAVE THEM DO UNTO YOU.

THERE was a lake on whose green banks grew many pretty flowers. Beautiful Dryope, with her smiling baby in her arms, loved to carry garlands of roses to the water-nymphs who lived in the lake. Once when wandering there she found a lotus blossom and broke it from the stem to give it to her baby for a plaything.

Dryope's sister, who was with her, looked at the blossom and was much frightened to see drops of blood where the stem was broken off. The tree was trembling too, as if shaken with horror. It was a tree which had once been a lovely maiden by the name of Lotis. But being pursued by a wooer whom she did not like, Lotis had changed into a flowery plant.

When Dryope saw the lotus bleeding and trembling, she humbly begged it to forgive her, and then she tried to run away, but she could not. She found that her feet had roots like a plant, and that the roots had grown down into the ground and held her fast. She tried to get away, but could not. Something like the bark of a tree began to grow around her. She put her hands up to her head and found that her hair had turned to leaves.

She pressed her baby to her heart, but her arms began to turn into branches, like the branches of a tree. Poor Dryope now knew that she too must become a tree. She gave her baby to her sister, and asked her to let him come and play under her branches when he grew to be a boy.

She said she hoped he would never break off a branch from a tree lest it might be the home of a goddess or nymph. And she begged her sister never to let the cows and sheep bite off her tender branches, or eat her leaves, since that would give her great pain. Thus perished Dryope crying out that she was unjustly punished.

Spelling.

lotus   frightened   Lotis   Dry o′pe

Topics for discussion.

The sin of insensibility. The practice of ruthlessly destroying plants. Care of flowers and trees. Arbor Day. Have trees any rights? Any feelings? The sensitive plant. Proofs that plants can feel injuries. Influence of trees on climate. How can you tell one tree from another? With what trees are you acquainted? What can you tell about them? Over what extent the roots spread. At what height above ground the branches begin.

Note.

Lowell's poem "Rhoecus" is an interesting study in connection with this lesson.

LESSON XXIII.

THE CRANES OF IBYCUS.

SEVERAL old writers mention a race of little men called Pygmies, who lived far away toward the rising of the sun. These little people were afraid of some large birds called cranes, which had long bills and immense appetites. The Pygmies and the cranes had great battles, in which the little people were often beaten and eaten.

After awhile the birds came together by common consent in a great council, and it was agreed that they should all fly away. They formed in ranks like an army, put guards in the rear to keep the army in order and not let any weaker ones get lost. Then they appointed a leader, and rising high into the air where they could see far off into the distance and choose the pleasantest land, they set off with great screams.

It was evening when they started. They flew all night, and rested in the day-time, when they hid themselves in tall grasses in marshy places. They appointed day-guards to watch while they slept. They put a stone in the claw of each guard and told him that he would be punished if he let it fall.

When the guards were appointed, the birds tucked their heads under their wings, each standing on one foot, and dropped off into a slumber. It is said that they slept all day, and when night came they flew on again, so that no one should see them flying, and that they carried their crops full of sand, and stones in their claws to steady them in their flight, as a ship carries ballast.

As they journeyed along, they looked down one bright moonlight night and saw a wandering musician, a minstrel, singing from door to door. He sang such songs as the birds sing, and the cranes stopped in their flight to listen. Ibycus, for that was the wanderer's name, had started out to attend a chariot race, where all the tribes of the country came once a year to a festival. Here the poets met and the singers; and those who sang the sweetest songs were crowned with pine. Ibycus had learned his music from Apollo, the god of music, who was said to understand all harmonies, and to play on a harp with golden strings.

When Ibycus left the town and entered the forest, he began to be afraid, for he did not know the way. But looking upward, he saw the gray squadron moving swiftly through the skies, and he called out, "Hail to thee, friendly band! I deem it a favorable sign that thou too art come from a distant coast, and dost go in the same direction with me."

Ibycus hastened on in a joyous mood, and soon reached a little bridge where he was attacked by two robbers, who came to steal the gifts which travellers laid on the altars of the gods that were all about the groves. They were rough fellows, unable to understand the gentle poet, whose hand could tune the lyre, but could not string the deadly bow. The poet struggled to free himself, and cried out for help, but no one came to his assistance. Then he called to the cranes, " Bear ye my dying song to the festival." And he lay down and died of the wounds the robbers had inflicted.

The news of the poet's death was received with great grief at the festival, and all the people hastened to pour wine on the ground that the spirit of the dead man might be at peace and pass to the happy fields of Elysium. But there was a band

A FURY.

of furies who circled in a stately dance, chanting fearful songs of sorrow for the beloved Ibycus.

Suddenly the heavens became black as night, and a voice cried out, "See there! See there! Behold the cranes!" When the robbers saw the cranes, they were seized with trembling, and gave themselves up to punishment.

Spelling.

pygmies	council	Ib'y cus
inflicted	appetites	appointed
squadron	favorable	elysium

Note to Teachers.

For the original of this story, see "Stories from Pliny for Boys and Girls," by Dr. John S. White. There are many of Pliny's Stories that are interesting for primary reading.

Topics for discussion.

Why birds migrate. When. Why in armies. Why they all start at once. John Burroughs says "Perhaps they have a sixth sense. It is not true that they have a leader."

Historic discussion.

Practice of the ancient Greeks in assembling at Corinth for festivals. Their practice of leaving gifts on altars. What historic truth in the story? Separate the truth from the fiction.

LESSON XXIV.

THE PIPER WHO PIPES ON SEVEN REEDS.

I REMEMBER a little boy who used to make a great many whistles. He did not live in a city where he could go to a store and buy all the whistles he wanted, as most children can; but that was

not any matter, for he learned a
great many things in making his
own whistles, that other children
who buy whistles will never know.
This little boy's name was Ned,
and he lived in a country town
where there were not many other
boys, and he had to amuse himself.

Ned lived on a hill, and there
was quite a large pond just down
back of the hill, with many willow
trees growing all about.   Ned used
to go down to the pond to play,
and he often cut off a willow
branch and made whistles from it.
This is how he did it.   He took
the branch while it was fresh and
green, cut it up into short sticks
and put them into the pond so that

they would not dry up. Then he took one of the sticks and knocked it gently on all sides until the bark was loose and he could slip it off. He cut a little hole through the bark into the wood and slipped the bark off, and cut a groove in the wood. Then he slipped the bark on again without breaking it, and there was a beautiful whistle, as fine as any boy would want.

Sometimes Ned picked pumpkin vines and made whistles of them also, queer whistles that sounded like deep hollow voices; and he found hollow reeds growing in the pond, from which he made musical whistles, and he made fiddles from corn-stalks.

These things country boys can do because they live where things grow, and it makes me think of a story about some one who was said to be a god of music, the music that comes from reeds and grasses and pine trees and all those things that grow out of doors.

For my part, I am not sure there ever was any such creature. It might have been a good, smart boy like Ned, who wore clothes made of the skins of goats and made whistles out of willows and vines and all sorts of wild things, just a shepherd lad tending his sheep in lonely places by river sides and lake sides, singing and whistling and dancing to keep up his spirits.

But people called him god Pan, and they said that he was half goat and half man, that he had the head and arms of a man, but that the lower half of his body was that of a goat. He wore the horns of a goat on his head, and he carried a shepherd's staff and invented musical instruments. When evening came, and the gentle winds made music among the vines and trees, people said, "God Pan is piping out among the reeds."

And when the beautiful spring came with its pink buds they said, "God Pan is dancing in the forests like the frisky goat on the mountain," and when the babbling streams ran along, their music mingling with the melodies of the breezes among the leaves, the people said, "God Pan and his companions, the frisky satyrs, are scaring the water-nymphs, the goddesses who live in the murmuring streams."

It happened that there was a beautiful land where the mountains rose into the white clouds, the valleys were garlanded with green, and dancing rivulets ran singing along among bushes covered with white syringa blossoms. Here the wild stag bounded over the hillside, and nymphs bathed in the brooks, the air blew more softly and sweetly in the summer, and people were happy and worshipped god Pan.

Here the beautiful Hamadryads wandered, the spirits who lived in trees and bushes, living while they lived, and dying when they died.

Among the Hamadryads, who haunted the syringa bushes on the banks of one of the pretty streams, lived a water-nymph whose name was Syrinx, and I think the name of the syringa blossom would have been forgotten long ago if it had not been so much like hers.

Syrinx, or Syringa I will call her, was often frightened by the companions of god Pan, the goat-

men who danced around on the
hills, frisking about on their goat-
legs, and piping merry tunes on
their reed-whistles. They were
naughty fellows, those goat-men,
as naughty as some big boys are
nowadays, who love to chase little

girls and frighten
them, and laugh to see
them run. Neverthe-
less Syringa dressed
herself up like a hunt-
ress, and took a golden bow and
went about over the hills hunting
the deer and the rabbit, and when
the people saw her they cried,
"There is Diana, the hunter
goddess who lives in the country
of the quails."

One day when she was out roaming about the woods and hills, god Pan saw her. He was coming home from one of his revels, frisking along like a goat, his head all covered with sharp pine leaves. And when he saw Syringa, he thought he would like to have her dance at his revels, and frisk about over the hills with him and be his play-fellow. So he ran after her, calling to her; but she was frightened when she saw the goat-like creature, and she fled from him over the hills and through the bushes where there were no paths, until she came to a gentle stream whose banks were covered with reeds and syringa bushes.

The stream was too broad for her to cross over, so she prayed to the water-nymphs to change her into some other form that Pan might not catch her.

The nymphs heard her prayer, and turned her into a syringa bush covered with blossoms whiter than milk.

When god Pan caught her, he found his arms full of great branches of the syringa bush, with its white flowers glowing like a beautiful face. And, as he stood there mourning over his loss, he heard a murmuring noise, a sweet, sad, low tone like one complaining, coming from the branches of the syringa; for the syringa, like the willow, has a hollow tube which is musical.

God Pan was charmed with the sweet voice, and he said, "Syringa, thou hast escaped me, but thy whispers are sweeter than thyself.

Thy soul doth come to me through this hollow branch. This way of conversing with thee shall ever remain to me. Oh, the delight of speaking to thee through music."

Then he took seven branches
and bound them together, and
made them into a musical
instrument of seven pipes. And
he often sat on the banks of the
gentle stream, among the syringa
blossoms playing on the pipe of
seven reeds. And when the people
heard the music off by the river,
they said, "God Pan is piping
down among the rushes. He is
holding conversation with the
beautiful Syringa."

I love to think of god Pan
piping by the river, and I love to
think of Ned piping down by the
pond, and I believe that any one
who might see a beautiful stream
dancing down the mountain, hiding

itself among syringa bushes, with frisky goats scampering along its banks, would feel like telling this story, whether he believed it or not.

Spelling.

Syringa	conversing	reeds
Hamadryads	piping	reads
satyr	dancing	

Topics for discussion.

Separation of the myth from the nature story. How much of the story is true? Which is history?

Dress of the ancients. Invention of musical instruments. The syringa.

LESSON XXV.

WHAT PLATO SAID ABOUT THE SPHERE.

A LITTLE boy was told that he might do anything he pleased, and this is what he did. He helped himself to a large handful of clay and sat down and made it into a beautiful sphere, which was admired very much. But after awhile we looked again, and the little boy had put a big nose onto his sphere and some eyes and lips, and he had attached long arms with hands of amazing size, and legs and feet. He told us that it was a man, but we thought it was a wild fellow. One would suppose that a sphere with legs and feet would run away, but the little boy said that his sphere kept rolling around until he gave it feet so that it could stand still.

The Sphere Family is a strange company. It is said that everything in the universe would like to be a sphere. Apples and oranges try to be round. Cherries, and blueberries, and snowballs, and sleighbells, and marbles, try their best to look like spheres. Ages ago, when everything used to be a gas, even that went whirling round and round until it came together in shape of a ball, which rolled over and over until it had thrown off a countless number of smaller balls,

which turned out to be suns, and
moons, and stars, and the earth on
which we live. It seems to be the
nature of everything that has
nothing on which to stand, to go
whirling around and turn into balls
just like the universe.

When rain falls from the clouds,
the drops turn round and round and
become little spheres. When they
freeze we call them hail-stones.
Molten lead, dropped from the top
of a shot tower, falls at the base in
balls which we call shot. But
Plato told a story about a sphere
which is more marvelous than any
of these stories.

Long before man lived on the
earth or had a body, he had a Mind

or Spirit. The Mind or Spirit was good and holy. It could see the truth, and understand the truth, and love the truth. It came from the Creator of the universe. He created the seed which should produce it, and gave it to the gods, and made it immortal. And he told them to weave this immortal part into a mortal body, because the mind would need contact with objects to become wise.

Now, when the gods saw the universe, that it was full of spheres, and that these spheres moved around each other, and around the sun, all in the greatest harmony, they thought it would be quite proper to create a body for Man on

the same plan, and so they made a
head, in which he might carry his
Mind. They made it in the form
of a ball, and said that since it was
the part of him which recognized
justice and truth, it should be the
lord over all that was in Man.

But the head could not get on
very well all alone. It could do
nothing but go rolling every which
way, unless something helped it to
stand still.   So the gods gave all
the rest of the body to it, to be its
servant, in order that it might not
tumble about among the deep and
high places of the earth, but might
be able to get across ditches without falling in, and over mountains
without tumbling down.   They

placed the head at the top of the
body, so that each man might carry
his Mind high up above everything
base. And so it became the temple
of the holy Spirit, the dwelling-
place of the most sacred and divine
part of us. The arms were attached
merely to take care of the head,
and the trunk to support it, and
the legs to carry it.

Each side of a sphere seems to
be exactly like every other side,
but the gods easily told one side
from another, for they considered
the front more honorable than the
back. So they put a nose on the
front of it, and a mouth also, with
lips and teeth. They put ears on
the right side and left, and hair on

the back, and gave the whole body a forward motion. And they contrived the eyes, to give light to the head, so that it could have all the fire it needed, but not enough to burn it up.

The gift of the eyes was very important, for it enabled the head to see the sun, moon, and stars. If it had not been for that, the head could never have told night from day, nor summer from winter, nor one month from another, because the sun makes the day and the night, and measures off the year, while the moon measures off the month.

God gave us eyes for this reason, that we might behold the

intelligence in the heaven, how great it is, how serene and undisturbed, and that we might apply it to our own intelligence, and become serene and happy.

Spelling.

sphere   universe   immortal   created
contrived   intelligence   measures   attached

Topics for discussion.

Type forms, the sphere, cube, cylinder, cone, etc. Why the sphere is considered the most beautiful of them all. Objects based on the sphere. Objects based on other type forms. Why the study of type forms is essential in education. "He who is best creates only the fairest, and it must be like himself." The Mind. Its right to serenity and composure. The serenity of Socrates and Plato. Their habits of ignoring the petty externalities which make up the happiness of "low-minded" people. The habit of high-mindedness.

Note.

This story can be found in Timaeus of Plato.

LESSON XXVI.

ATLANTIS, THE LOST ISLAND.

IT often happens that some little
boy says, " I wish I were rich,"
thinking that if he had a great deal
of money he could buy, for his own
enjoyment, all the toys and candies
and good clothes that heart could
desire.   It is very easy to forget
that " the earth is the Lord's and
the fulness thereof," and that no
one on the earth can be any richer
than any other person, except by
being more deeply in debt.   It is
easy to imagine that if we had
money or lands they would be our
own, but this must look quite

absurd to Him who has lent us His goods for a few years to use as if they were our own, for the welfare of all.

It is quite certain that Plato believed that a man's true riches were in his Mind and not outside of him ; that a man was rich who had the power to get money, and the power and will to use it well for others, — the ability and will being all the riches there were about it ; and that that man was the richest of all who did not care for riches. Plato hoped to make his fellow citizens see that the love of money and a show of wealth were vulgar, so he told them the story of a lost island.

Long ages ago, the gods had the whole earth. Each one knew what was proper for himself to have, so no one tried to get more than was his share, and each one put as many people on his own land as could be happy there.

When the gods had peopled their districts, they tended human beings as good shepherds tend their flocks, not by driving them, or striking them, but like guides who go ahead to show the way. Each god loved his own people, and set his own kingdom in order.

Athena was the Goddess of Wisdom, and she loved learning and hard work. She knew how to spin and weave, and make wise laws, and conquer in battle. She chose for her subjects only brave people, and she put patriotism into their hearts, and gave them noble natures.

They did not care for riches, or desire to live in palaces, but they built small houses, in which they lived and grew old. They built splendid temples in which to worship, and fine public houses, for they loved the gods and their country better than they loved themselves. There were only twenty thousand of these people, but they were so strong that they could not be conquered by a million soldiers.

The god of the waters, Poseidon, had quite a different kingdom. He received for his portion the island of Atlantis, and he married Cleito, a mortal woman, and settled down in a pretty part of the island. On the side toward the sea, and in the centre of the island, there was a fertile plain which was very beautiful. There was a low mountain running across the island, about seven miles from the sea, and it kept off the cold north winds, so that the long south slope, where most of the people lived, was warm and pleasant. Poseidon loved Cleito so much that he resolved to surround her home with embankments and canals so high and deep that no other king could come and carry her off. So he broke the ground all round the hill on which she dwelt, making a high belt of earth in the form of a ring which encircled her, and outside of that was a ring of water, so wide that it looked like a sea. Then came another ring of land, and another ring of water, affording such a protection to the princess that no one could ever hear anything about her, and no ship could get into the rings of water, and no man could get to the island. Poseidon contrived to supply the island with fresh water by bringing up two streams from under the earth. He caused them to come up as fountains, one of warm water and one of cold, and he made every variety of food to spring up from the earth.

Poseidon and Cleito had ten sons, five pairs of twins, and each son received a part of the kingdom as his own. The oldest son, Atlas, became king of the island, and named it after himself, Atlantis, and he gave the name to the Atlantic Ocean. He was a large, strong man, and it is said that he held up the sky and plucked the golden apples.

The people of the empire of Atlas became very rich. They brought many things from foreign countries. They dug gold and silver out of their mines. They cut valuable wood from their forests.

They had elephants, and horses, and oxen, and all other kinds of tame animals and wild animals, every sort that can live in mountains or plains, or in lakes, marshes, rivers, canals, and ditches. And they had roots, and herbs, and flowers, and fruit, and everything to eat and drink in infinite abundance. They spent their time in building docks, and harbors, and bridges, and temples, and palaces, until everything was a marvel of luxury and beauty. They built a stone wall around one embankment, with towers and gates, and they covered the next one with tin, and the outer one with brass. They built a temple to Poseidon over six

hundred feet long, and covered the
pinnacles with silver and gold.
They ornamented the roof with
ivory, and gold, and silver, and
lined the floor with a precious
metal. In the temple they placed
statues of gold. There was one
of Poseidon himself standing in a
chariot, driving six winged horses
— it was of such a size that his head
touched the roof. And around it
were a hundred water-nymphs
riding on dolphins' backs. There
were images and golden statues of
kings and their wives; there were
fountains, and trees, and cisterns,
and the king's bath, and baths for
women, and baths for men, and
baths for horses and cattle; there

were aqueducts, race-courses, guard-
houses, naval stores, ships, and
such a crowd of rich, elegant, lazy,
proud people, charioteers, fighters,
archers, slingers, stone-shooters,
skirmishers, pugilists, that it would
be tiresome to mention them. The
ten kings had absolute control of
the city and country. They made
the laws, and drove the people
about like slaves, striking, punish-
ing, and slaying any one whom
they disliked. Now, to people who
had no eyes to see the truth,
these wretched folks still appeared
glorious and blessed at the very
time when they were filled with
avarice and riches. But they began
to appear base to those who had

eyes to see truly. They had lost their most precious riches, they had been unable to bear up under good fortune, for their lower natures had become their masters. Then they began to look at the little kingdom ruled over by Athena, where the people loved hard work and virtue, and were very comfortable in poverty. And they saw that the divinity of their own natures had become diluted by being mixed with wealth.

So the god of Atlantis directed his great power against the little kingdom of Athena, and there the story ends, but it is easy enough to guess the rest of it; for the island of Atlantis, if there ever was one, has sunk beneath the sea.

It does not make a grain of difference whether there ever was an Atlantis or not. Plato's story was just as true as if he had said, "There will be a Roman Empire, which will fall because its people will love riches better than virtue."

The principle always holds. No nation can stand except through the uprightness and simplicity of its citizens.

"When men are good and true, and stand shoulder to shoulder, a nation is strong; it is strong in its quantity of life, and not in its lands or gold.

A thing is worth what it can do for you; not what you pay for it.

The wealth of a nation depends upon the number it can employ in making good and useful things.

Peace of heart, contentedness in simple employments, these are a nation's wealth."

Spelling.

| Atlantis | A the′ na | simplicity |
| Po sei′ (sī) don | Clei′ to | principle |

Topics for discussion

The rising and sinking of coasts, islands, continents (see Guyot's " Earth and Man "). The probability that there was such an island as Atlantis. Proofs. The ethical point intended by Plato. Patriotism. What examples in American history of heroes who have sacrificed wealth to national needs? Lafayette. Franklin.

Note.

See Plato's " Republic " and " The Critias."

LESSON XXVII.

PRINCE RED CAP.

THERE was once a prince who wore a red cap, and he was a famous drummer. He drummed on trees and on stones, or most anything, and made music come out of any sort of a stick or grass-blade or stump or knot-hole.

He was so beautiful that everything loved him. The wood-nymphs whispered to him through the reeds and pine-needles, the willows bent down and murmured their complaints to him, the water-nymphs sang to him from streams and fountains, and he was as popular as a gold dollar.

But Prince Red Cap was deaf to all the voices in the woods. He had heard the voice of a singer who lived on the Hill of the Palaces, and he said, "This maiden has gathered all the sweet sounds into her own voice, all the music of the leaves and the branches and of the streams that babble."

Wonderful, indeed, as she was in her beauty, she was yet more wonderful in her singing, and so she was called Canens. At the sound of her voice the trees would leap from the ground and the rocks dance with gladness. Long rivers stopped running that they might hear her magical notes, and the wild beasts became tame in order to listen to her singing.

One day as Canens was singing in her home, Prince Red Cap mounted his horse and rode out to hunt the wild boars that lived in the forests and fields all around the Hill of the Palaces. He wore a purple cloak fastened with yellow clasps, and he carried two javelins in his left hand. As he went along he kept drumming on everything with his javelins to please himself.

Now, it happened that same day that a golden-haired princess, who was the daughter of the Sun and Ocean, had come out into a field that she might gather some fresh flowers. She was standing just back of a shrub as Prince Red Cap came riding along, and she was so astonished at his beauty that all the flowers she had gathered fell out of her hands.

Before she could pick them up Prince Red Cap had been borne far away by his swift horse, and he stood surrounded by his guards, talking about the boar he wanted to kill, and wondering where to find him. Then the sunny-faced princess, who was something of a witch, too, plucked a magic blossom, which she turned into the image of a wild boar, and she commanded it to run through the fields right in front of Prince Red Cap, and to seem to come back to a forest close by. This forest was so packed with shrubs that no horse could enter it.

So the little phantom boar ran more swiftly than the winds right in front of Prince Red Cap, and when he saw it he gave chase and rode full tilt after it, until he came to the edge of the forest. When he

found he could not enter on horse-
back he left his horse and ran after
the phantom. And as he ran he
came close to the witch, the daughter of the Sun.

Then she said to
him, "O Beautiful Prince, cease
to chase that boar, and sit down
and let me admire you. You
are running after a phantom.
Leave the phantom and help me

gather flowers. I will take you to
my father, the Sun. He is the
source of Light. He will admire
you, too, and love you, and teach
you great mysteries. He will show
you how to see into all secret things,
and how to find everything that is
hidden. You shall live in his palace,
and be a king in his golden halls,
and he may even fancy you for a
son-in-law."

Prince Red Cap bowed politely
and said, " Really, I beg your par-
don, but I don't remember your
name. Your face is bright and
sunny. One would live in summer-
land all the time if he married you.
But I have promised to return to
Canens, the daughter of Winter.

She is a sweet singer and her voice calls me. She is waiting for me, and she has promised to be my wife."

The daughter of the Sun turned herself to the West, and her face looked like a golden cloud at the setting of the sun. And she turned herself to the East, and she looked like the rosy morning. She touched Prince Red Cap with her wand, and said: "Beautiful Prince, you shall never return to Canens. You shall be my bird, and live in my fields, where your beauty may delight my father's heart and mine also."

Then Prince Red Cap turned and fled, but he did not get on very fast, and he wondered what was the matter. He looked down and saw that he had wings, and he soon found that he was changed into a strange bird with a red head. He had become a woodpecker. He was very angry, and perched on an old dead limb and began to drum for his guards. Then he flew to a fine live branch and struck the bark so hard that he wounded the branch. His wings took on the color of the purple robe he had worn. His bright golden buckle became a band of yellow feathers, and nothing remained to him of his former self except his name, and there was not much in that.

In the meantime his companions went searching through the forest, calling, "Picus! Picus! Red Cap! Red Cap!" but they could not find him. They found his horse standing where he had left it, near the shining goddess, and they accused her of changing their prince into some monster and hiding him, and they attacked her with spears.

Then the daughter of the Sun gathered together the gods of Night. From the depths of black darkness she called them, and she howled at the moon and it came to aid her, and there was a great storm. The trees leapt out from the forests, the ground uttered groans, the grass was sprinkled with blood, the stones seemed to speak in tones like the lowing of cattle, the dogs barked, the ground was covered with crawling things, and phantoms flitted about. The people were astonished and trembled. Then the goddess touched some of the young men with her wand and the forms of wild beasts came upon them.

That night, when the sun was going down, Canens, the sweet singer, looked in vain for her prince to return. So she summoned her people and they went forth with lanterns and torches to meet him. But they could not find him. Then Canens wandered over the fields for six days and six nights searching for Prince Red Cap, going, without food and without sleep, over hills and valleys, wherever chance led her. At last she came to a river and sat down upon its banks. And she sang a low, sweet song, such as the swan sings when it is about to die. She poured forth her heart in this melody, growing weaker and weaker, until by degrees she was changed into the thin blue air which is heard in the music of the pine leaves and supports the bird in its flight.

And it is quite certain that Prince Red Cap still remembers her sweet voice as he hears the zephyrs whispering to him while he hammers away in the oak trees and the apple trees. He is very cross to Mrs.

Woodpecker and drives her away. When he builds a new house he lets Mrs. Woodpecker live in the old one. In the spring he sits and drums and drums for a mate, and when one comes he keeps on drumming, and it is more than likely that he believes that Canens will come if he only drums long enough.

This story teaches that a gold belt and a red cap and a purple cloak and other kinds of fine clothes may make a fine bird, but they do not make a fine man. And I am sure we all pity poor Picus and wish he had left his gay clothes at home and had had the good sense to wear plain ones, for he had a good heart and deserved a better fate. And the story teaches another lesson about little phantom boars that run along as if they were real boars. It is better to keep right at one's own work than to try to kill them.

Spelling.

popular   phantom   valleys   vibrates

magical   valley   javelins   opinion

Topics for discussion.

The real meaning of the story. Its interpretation as a nature story. The woodpecker. Plumage. Habit of drumming. The phantom boar. Pursuit of trifles or low ideals. The Palatine Hill.